The Inner Child Recovery Workbook

Move On From the Past, Address Abandonment Trauma, and Achieve Emotional Freedom

Samantha Parker

© Copyright 2025 – Samantha Parker – All rights reserved.

The content within this book may not be reproduced, duplicated, or transmitted without direct written permission from the author and/or the publisher.

Under no circumstances will any blame or legal responsibility be held against the author and/or publisher, for any damages, reparation, or monetary loss due to the information contained within this book, either directly or indirectly.

Legal Notice

This book is copyright-protected. It is for personal use only. You cannot amend, distribute, sell, use, or paraphrase any part, or the content within this book, without the consent of the author and/or publisher.

Disclaimer Notice

Please note that the information contained within this document is for educational and entertainment purposes only. All effort has been executed to present accurate, up-to-date, reliable, and complete information. No warranties of any kind are declared or implied. Readers acknowledge that the author is not rendering legal, financial, medical, or professional advice.

Table of Contents

Introduction 5

Chapter 1: Revisiting Our Past 7

    Your Personal Retreat 8

    Create a Personal Trigger 10

Chapter 2: What Is the Inner Child? 22

    Inner Child Archetypes 23

    Exploring the Depths of the Psyche 25

    Reconnection With Your Inner Child 27

Chapter 3: Childhood Influence on Adult Life 38

    The Impact of Childhood on Relationships 39

    The Impact of Childhood on Work 39

    Embracing and Healing Your Inner Child 40

    Embracing Your True Self 41

Chapter 4: Defining Your Personal Space 57

    Physical Boundaries 58

    Emotional Boundaries 59

    Time Boundaries 60

    Financial Boundaries 61

    The Impact of Unclear Boundaries 64

    Inner Child and Boundaries 65

How to Set Healthy Boundaries 67

Defining and Communicating Personal Boundaries 69

Confronting Discomfort 69

Your Voice Matters 82

Chapter 5: Reparenting Your Inner Child **83**

Nurturing Your Inner Child 85

Speaking to Your Inner Child 86

Gardening the Self 88

Managing Life's Expectations 89

Chapter 6: Emotions and Childhood **98**

Identifying and Controlling Emotions 100

Emotional Intelligence 102

Chapter 7: From Surviving to Thriving **111**

Transforming Your Inner Dialogue 112

Levels of Change 115

Overcoming Perfectionism 116

Dream Big 119

A Final Note 129

Conclusion **130**

About the Author **133**

Introduction

There is an almost imperceptible moment just before the world spins out of control. It is that split second before your morning coffee spills as you slam on the brakes because someone cut you off on the highway, or the instant you notice your usual parking spot is taken and realize today is going to be challenging. Let us discuss those moments because they are not as isolated as they appear. They are signs of a deeper malaise—a signal from your inner self begging for attention.

Anna is having one of those days. Traffic is a nightmare, her coffee has stained her blouse, and her inbox contains an ominous message from her boss: "We need to talk about your project." These incidents might seem trivial individually, but their cumulative weight is overwhelming. Normally, Anna is not shaken by such things, but today, something inside her is ready to burst.

Many might dismiss these as simply bad days, but they often serve as our mind's way of signaling a problem. It is like a younger version of ourselves, neglected for too long, tugging at our adult life, demanding attention. Ignoring this inner voice does not heal its wounds; it merely silences it temporarily.

Take Anna's response, for instance. Instead of spiraling, she chooses to address the root cause of her distress. This change in strategy is not about fighting external irritations but rather confronting the internal reverberations from her past. We all have an inner child—an idea that is not new but deeply significant. This inner child lives within us, holding onto the joys and traumas of our early years. For some, these traumas are profound and scarring; for others, they are subtle, barely noticeable moments that have nonetheless shaped their emotional world.

Facing these memories is not about changing the past—it is about altering how we engage with the present. Healing our inner child does not just mend old wounds; it changes our perception of the world and our place within it. This process is neither quick nor easy, but it is transformative. It enables us to approach life not as victims of our past but as creators of our future.

Anna began by acknowledging her feelings, and recognizing them as valid and important. She realized that her overreactions were not signs of weakness but indicators of unresolved emotions. This insight did not come from an external source; it emerged from engaging in a dialogue with her younger self, a conversation many of us silence as we grow older.

The journey truly begins with such acknowledgments. For Anna, this meant embracing journaling as a tool for communicating with her inner child, allowing her to express fears and frustrations without self-criticism. These writings were not elaborate or structured; they were authentic, unfiltered, and incredibly therapeutic.

In addition, she adopted mindfulness techniques, which enabled her to observe her reactions without immediate judgment or action. This space between feeling and response became the realm of healing, offering her the freedom to choose her reaction rather than being controlled by initial impulses.

Through these practices, Anna discovered peace and gained clarity and a fresh perspective on daily challenges. Her morning commutes shifted from being solely about traffic to moments of reflection and preparation for the day ahead, fostering a sense of tranquility amid life's chaos.

This journey is not about burying the past or ignoring the pain. It is about coming to terms with it, gleaning lessons from it, and ultimately, forging ahead with newfound resilience. Our inner child is not a burden to be silenced but a companion on life's journey—someone who reminds us of our origins and guides us toward our destination.

So, to anyone grappling with unseen struggles, remember: The road to healing commences with a simple yet courageous act of listening to that inner child. Engage with them, comprehend their fears, comfort their wounds, and witness as the "adult you" begins to navigate life with a lighter stride and a clearer perspective.

Chapter 1:
Revisiting Our Past

Have you ever taken a stroll through your neighborhood, only to catch a delightful aroma that instantly transports you to a cherished moment from your past? Perhaps it is the smell of freshly baked cookies, reminiscent of cozy afternoons spent with your grandmother, or the enticing scent of barbecue, evoking memories of summer evenings with family. Scents possess a magical quality that can tether us to memories, thanks to the intricate way our senses capture and recall experiences.

Our senses serve as portals to the past, adeptly storing memories with rich, multi-sensory details, allowing a mere aroma or touch to unleash a cascade of memories. For instance, the softness of a plush teddy bear might conjure the joy of receiving a cherished toy as a child.

However, not all sensory triggers evoke pleasant memories. Consider the sound of a school bell, for example. Recently, I accompanied my son to a "mock class" at his school, anticipating an exciting day of exploring his new surroundings and meeting his teachers. As we laughed and discussed his expectations for the upcoming school year, it was a truly special moment for both of us.

However, the moment the bell chimed, I was whisked back to my own school days. My heart raced, and I felt the familiar urgency of rushing between classes, coupled with the occasional dread of being unprepared. Does anyone else relate to this? Suddenly, I was not fully present with my son; I was immersed in memories of my youth. Unintentionally, I found myself hurriedly guiding him from one classroom to another, scarcely absorbing the teachers' explanations of the year ahead.

This encounter highlighted the profound influence our surroundings and their associated sensory triggers can have on our behavior and emotions. If a simple sound can evoke such vivid recollections of past anxieties, imagine how intentionally shaping our environments can help cultivate the emotions we desire to experience.

In the journey of healing and reconnecting with our inner child, it is imperative to establish a space that embodies tranquility, safety, and comfort. This nurturing environment is crucial for confronting and processing intense emotions and memories. Not only does such a space provide respite from the daily stresses of life, but it also facilitates the cultivation of a loving and supportive relationship with our inner child. By aligning our surroundings with our emotional needs, we lay the groundwork for profound internal healing and personal growth.

Your Personal Retreat

Your personal retreat can be as simple as a cozy corner in your home—a cherished chair or a cushioned spot where you feel completely relaxed. The size or grandeur of the space is not crucial; what matters is that it serves as a sanctuary for your mind, body, and spirit.

When setting up your personal retreat, consider a few essentials. Privacy is paramount. The exercises in this book may evoke deep emotions, and having a private space ensures you can explore these feelings without interruption. If possible, choose a location where you can close a door to indicate to others that you require uninterrupted time. Even a small area can be effective.

Reflect on what enhances or detracts from your sense of tranquility in this space. Perhaps adorn the area with photographs that evoke feelings of love and peace, and avoid clutter such as piles of unsorted mail, which could heighten stress. Personalizing this space is crucial; it should reflect your essence and promote a feeling of safety and calm. Whether through the comforting presence of plants, the softness of curtains, the grounding energy of crystals, or the gentle illumination of candles, make it a place that authentically represents you.

If possible, try to keep this area free from electronic devices. Disconnecting from constant digital notifications can significantly heighten your sense of peace. Grant yourself permission to step away from the digital buzz of phones, computers, and TVs, and observe how this aids in reconnecting with yourself.

With your physical sanctuary in place, let us turn our attention to cultivating another essential space—the internal haven you will nurture within.

Our most profound transformations often unfold not in the tangible world but within the realms of our minds. To facilitate this, it is vital to develop a mental space that is as real and comforting as any physical room. Your mind possesses an extraordinary capacity to conjure places of tranquility and safety—spaces where you feel secure, relaxed, and content, whether rooted in reality or born from the boundless realms of imagination.

Begin by envisioning your ideal peaceful setting. What landscapes bring solace to your soul? Is it the serene quiet of a forest, the rhythmic lapping of ocean waves at a beach, or perhaps the cozy embrace of a grand library with endless shelves and a snug chair? Whether a familiar place or a fantastical retreat, the possibilities are endless. Start by gathering images or pictures that resonate with you, considering what each evokes within you. Is it the gentle sunlight filtering through leaves, the familiar creak of a porch swing, or the particular hue of a room that draws you in? Identify these elements—they are the foundation of your mental sanctuary.

Once inspired, find a comfortable spot to relax. This exercise involves a bit of daydreaming, so settle into a position that allows for easy drifting, whether with eyes open or closed. Imagine stepping into an empty, enchanted room—a space that morphs and expands according to your desires, perfectly tailored to your comfort. Populate this room with the elements you have chosen. If it is a beach, feel the sand beneath your feet, hear the seagulls overhead, and see the endless horizon. If a meadow, perhaps there is a blanket spread on the grass under the open sky. Engage all your senses. What textures surround you? What scents linger in the air? What sounds envelop you? The more detailed your visualization, the more tangible your mental sanctuary becomes.

As you immerse yourself in this space, observe how it affects your body. Do you feel a sense of joy or peace washing over you? Maybe there is a surprising sensation you did not expect. If something feels amiss, as it did for me initially with a cluttered space, make adjustments. Remove or alter elements until your physical response aligns with comfort and peace.

This mental haven now serves as a tool at your disposal, ready to be accessed whenever you need a moment of calm or respite from the chaos of the world. It is normal if visualizing your space proves challenging at first; clarity comes with practice. The more you visit, the more vivid and comforting your sanctuary will become. Each person's mental retreat is unique—what brings solace to one may not resonate with another. That is the beauty of this process; it is deeply personal and tailored to your individual needs. Now, let us explore how you can effortlessly access this sanctuary whenever you need it.

Create a Personal Trigger

Crafting a personal trigger entails creating a tactile cue that immediately links you to a desired mental state, akin to the serene mind-space we imagined earlier. This method, termed anchoring, establishes a tangible "button" on your body. When activated, it evokes a particular emotional or mental resource.

Now, let us reframe the process with a fresh structure and examples, ensuring it stands alone as a distinct piece:

1. **Define Your Desired Emotional State:** Begin by identifying the emotional state you wish to access swiftly. For this exercise, let us focus on cultivating a sense of peace akin to the tranquility of your envisioned mental sanctuary.

2. **Immerse Yourself in the Desired State:** Close your eyes and envision stepping into your mental sanctuary within your mind's eye. Engage all your senses as you immerse yourself in this serene environment—feel the gentle breeze against your skin, hear the soothing sounds of nature, and bask in the profound sense of calm. Allow this tranquil feeling to wash over you completely.

3. **Select a Unique Physical Touch Point:** Choose a distinct point on your body to serve as your anchor. This could be a subtle pinch on your wrist or a gentle tap on your collarbone—areas that you do not typically touch unconsciously throughout your day.

4. **Associate the Touch With Your Emotional State:** While fully immersed in the peaceful ambiance of your mental sanctuary, apply gentle pressure to your chosen touch point. Hold this touch for a few moments, allowing the sensation to merge with the emotional state of tranquility you are experiencing. This act solidifies the connection between the physical touch and your desired emotional state.

5. **Verify the Anchor's Effectiveness:** After briefly distracting yourself by engaging in a different activity or shifting your focus, revisit your touch point and activate it once more. Notice how quickly and effortlessly you can evoke the serene state associated with your mental sanctuary. This resurgence of peace confirms the effectiveness of your anchor in accessing your desired emotional state swiftly and reliably.

Regularly utilizing your anchor is essential for maintaining its effectiveness. Similar to a muscle, it strengthens with consistent use. This technique empowers you to summon positive states such as calm, motivation, or happiness swiftly, offering a valuable tool for emotional regulation and personal empowerment.

Every page you turn in this book marks progress on your journey toward self-recovery. Each effort you invest in healing and reconnecting with your inner self signifies advancement, even when immediate results may not be apparent. You are continuously moving forward in the right direction.

A crucial aspect of this journey involves creating a tranquil environment conducive to this delicate work. Addressing deep-seated emotions and nurturing your inner child becomes significantly more manageable when you are free from stress or emotional discomfort. Now that we have established methods for cultivating a serene atmosphere, the next phase entails inviting your inner child into this nurturing space to initiate the healing process.

Reflecting on Parental Relationships

Consider how your relationship with your parents has transformed over the years. Reflect on the changes from your childhood to the present and highlight key differences, both positive and negative.

Then	Now

Exploring Defenses in Inner Child Work

Many people tend to defend or rationalize painful childhood experiences, which can impede progress in healing your inner child.

This exercise aims to assist you in recognizing and exploring any defenses that might be obstructing your healing journey. Take a moment to contemplate the following questions:

In what ways might you be downplaying the traumatic experiences from your childhood?

_____

_____

_____

Are you normalizing behaviors or situations that were actually harmful or abnormal?

_____

_____

_____

Do you find yourself defending or protecting your caregivers out of fear, honor, guilt, or embarrassment?

_____

_____

_____

Are you consciously or unconsciously avoiding memories, thoughts, feelings, or emotions that are essential for your healing?

_____

_____

_____

Do you hold a belief that healing from these wounds is possible?

_____

_____

_____

Understanding Inner Child Triggers

As you forge a deeper connection with your inner child, you may find yourself becoming more sensitive to particular triggers.

This exercise is designed to aid you in examining and comprehending these triggers more thoroughly.

How frequently does your inner child feel triggered?

_____

_____

Identify the settings, times, and people involved when these triggers occur.

_____
_____
_____
_____
_____
_____

Do these triggers evoke memories of specific childhood experiences?

_____
_____
_____
_____
_____
_____

What are your immediate thoughts, feelings, or emotions when triggered?

_____
_____
_____
_____
_____
_____

Where in your body do you feel this activation?

_____
_____

When triggered, do you tend to react outwardly or withdraw? Explain why you think this happens.

_____
_____
_____
_____
_____
_____

What strategies can you employ to soothe your inner child when these triggers occur?

_____
_____
_____
_____
_____
_____

Inner Child Trigger Tracker

This table serves as a tool to track occurrences that activate your inner child, discern the reasons underlying these triggers, and document your reactions. Maintaining this record can assist in identifying patterns and devising strategies to effectively manage your responses.

Situation (who, what, when, where) *Document the details of the encounter or event that triggered your inner child.*	**Trigger Cause** *Explain the underlying reasons why this particular situation was triggering.*	**Reaction** *Describe how your inner child responded to the trigger.*

Revisiting Childhood Misconceptions

During childhood, we frequently lack the perspective and comprehension to fully grasp the complexities underlying our caregivers' actions. Yet, with maturity and insight, we gain the ability to revisit these moments and uncover the genuine motivations and circumstances that influenced our early experiences.

This exercise encourages you to contemplate any instances from your childhood where misunderstandings or misconceptions may have arisen and to reassess them with the understanding you have acquired since then.

Event	Childhood Perception	Current Understanding
Example: Parents got divorced.	I believed their divorce was my fault because I thought I had misbehaved.	Understanding later that they separated due to longstanding irreconcilable differences that existed well before I was born.

Event	Childhood Perception	Current Understanding

Reflecting on Harmful Childhood Messages

Demeaning Messages:
- "There is something wrong with you."
- "You cannot do anything right."
- "You are such a disappointment."
- "You are the reason I have so many problems."
- "No one cares what you think."
- "You are nothing but a burden."
- "You are more trouble than you are worth."

Messages That Unfairly Burden You:
- "You are my whole life."
- "You are the only one who cares about me."
- "You are the only one I can count on."
- "I need you so much — I could not make it without you."

Messages About Your Role:
- "It is your job to make me happy."
- "You have to earn my love."
- "You must obey, respect, and take care of me."
- "You have no right to disagree."

Reflect on these messages. Do any of them align with what you were told as a child? How have they impacted you?

_____
_____
_____
_____

Examining Childhood Messages

Based on your reflections from the previous exercise, think about the instances in your adult life when these detrimental childhood messages resurface. Consider ways you can actively dispute and overcome these false beliefs.

_____
_____
_____
_____
_____
_____
_____

Comforting Messages to Your Inner Child

Reflect on the comforting words or affirmations you needed from your caregivers during tough times as a child. What messages would have made you feel safe, secure, validated, comforted, and loved? Write these down and speak them aloud to your inner child, providing the support and reassurance you once needed.

_____
_____
_____
_____
_____
_____
_____

Exploring Joyful Childhood Memories

Reflect on your favorite age growing up. What made it special?

_____
_____
_____

Think about your childhood best friend. What qualities did they have that you appreciated the most?

_____
_____
_____

Identify who had the most significant positive influence on you during your childhood and describe how they impacted you.

_____
_____
_____

Recall your favorite childhood experience. What made it memorable?

_____
_____
_____

Make a list of everything you were thankful for as a child.

_____
_____
_____

Chapter 2:
What Is the Inner Child?

The inner child is a captivating element of your personality present since birth, storing all your early experiences, both joyful and painful. This part resides deep within your subconscious, often influencing your reactions and behaviors without your conscious awareness.

Consider your inner child as a direct connection to your childhood, occasionally steering your present-day decisions. Imagine if a child were making your daily choices—you might end up having ice cream for breakfast or impulsively reacting to work emails. While this can add spontaneity and fun to your life, allowing this childlike aspect to constantly take control could lead to chaos in your adult responsibilities.

Everyone has this inner aspect, which plays a crucial role in how we learn and grow. Your inner child holds your earliest beliefs, emotions, and memories, while also nurturing your hopes for the future. This part of your personality can bring playfulness to your day or unearth past traumas that hold you back.

For example, if you experienced neglect, disappointment, or trauma during your early years, these events leave lasting marks on your inner child. If these issues are not addressed, they can resurface as triggers in adulthood, impacting your behavior and emotional well-being.

Usually, our inner child remains dormant, allowing us to handle our daily lives smoothly. However, when something upsets this inner part—like a child not receiving a desired treat in a store—it becomes noticeable. It is important to pay attention to these signals. Your inner child might be showing signs of loneliness, seeking attention, or reacting to feelings of marginalization. These emotions often emerge in your adult life as moments when you feel overwhelmed or out of control.

The idea of the inner child is not just a modern concept; it traces back to the work of Carl Jung, a pioneering psychiatrist. Jung disputed the notion that we are born as blank slates. He introduced the concept of "Inner Child Archetypes" within our collective unconscious, suggesting that our personal development is deeply influenced by these archetypal figures. According to Jung, recognizing and engaging with these archetypes is crucial for personal growth.

To connect with and heal your inner child, it is helpful to identify which archetype primarily influences your behavior. Understanding this can empower you to reshape this archetype to better align with your adult goals and identity. As you read through this book, you will find tools and insights to help you engage with and transform your inner child, enabling a more harmonious integration of your past experiences with your present life.

Inner Child Archetypes

Archetypes, often called the shadow or dark side, are essential for comprehending our deeper selves. In this context, we will use the term "shadow" to indicate the negative aspects of these archetypes to avoid confusion, particularly with the specific archetype known as the wounded child.

The Wounded Child: This archetype represents individuals who have experienced trauma or severe hardship during their upbringing, often characterized by psychological or physical abuse. Such experiences usually result in defensive and distrustful behaviors in adulthood. People with a wounded inner child may find it challenging to form healthy relationships and may be at a higher risk of continuing abusive behaviors. However, when this archetype is recognized and healed, it can transform pain into profound empathy, bringing light and compassion to both oneself and others who have suffered.

The Orphaned Child: Marked by a strong attachment to independence, the orphaned child archetype arises from feelings of abandonment and emotional neglect. Such individuals may respond sharply to rejection and often withdraw from social interactions to shield themselves from further emotional pain. Healing this archetype enables one to embrace independence in a healthy manner, accept support gracefully, and cultivate a strong sense of self-reliance and intuition.

The Magical Child: The magical child finds wonder every day and believes in the interconnectedness of all things. This archetype is inherently intuitive and creative, often challenging conventional norms. However, if their imaginative spirit is suppressed or ridiculed during childhood, it can result in a disillusioned adult prone to depression and anxiety. Healing this archetype rekindles their belief in magic and possibility, allowing them to dream big and achieve their goals.

The Nature Child: The nature child archetype is profoundly linked to the natural world, discovering solace and happiness in outdoor environments and among animals. They frequently collect natural artifacts such as rocks and feathers. A shadow nature child might display disrespect toward nature and living beings, indicating a fractured bond with their environment. Healing aids in reestablishing their inherent connection with nature, cultivating a respectful and nurturing attitude toward both the environment and themselves.

The Eternal Child: The eternal child exudes youthfulness and enthusiasm, consistently marveling at the wonders of the world and deriving joy from life's simple pleasures. They possess a natural curiosity and excel at thinking outside the box. However, in its shadow manifestation, this archetype evades responsibility and grapples with the challenges of adult life, frequently relying on others for support. Healing promotes a harmonious balance, preserving their sense of joy while integrating mature coping mechanisms.

The Needy Child: Similar to the wounded and orphaned archetypes, the needy child seeks to fill an emotional void resulting from neglect. This archetype is continuously striving for fulfillment, propelled by a strong sense of justice and fairness. In its shadow aspect, they may seem self-centered, pursuing personal gain even in acts of altruism. Healing requires acknowledging and addressing these needs constructively, fostering a more balanced and reciprocal approach to relationships.

The Divine Child: Associated with spiritual or divine qualities, the divine child embodies purity and innocence at its core. They are often perceived as mystical and sought after for spiritual guidance or healing. However, in its shadow form, the divine child may misuse its influence, leading others astray or manipulating followers. Healing this archetype entails embracing genuine spirituality and utilizing its gifts for true benevolence, fostering a healthy and inspirational presence in the lives of others.

Understanding and nurturing these archetypes can result in profound personal growth and healing, enabling individuals to lead more fulfilling and balanced lives.

Exploring the Depths of the Psyche

Every individual carries a shadow self, a deeper aspect of their psyche that influences behaviors and emotional responses. Recognizing this shadow is crucial for personal growth and transformation. Take a moment to reflect on which aspects of the inner child archetypes evoke significant emotional reactions in you, whether positive or negative. These feelings act as signals from your subconscious, indicating areas that require attention. While you may resonate with multiple archetypes, focusing on the one that resonates most strongly can facilitate a more effective process of addressing and healing your shadow side.

For instance, suppose you find resonance with the archetype that thrives in natural settings but notice negative behaviors emerging during stressful situations. To realign with your inner self, immerse yourself in nature. This could involve taking walks in a park, interacting with wildlife, or simply sitting under a tree. These activities encourage a reconnection with your core self and provide a tranquil environment for introspection.

The origins of a shadow self often stem from unmet emotional needs during childhood, which may not necessarily be linked to overtly traumatic events. For example, if you required encouragement as a child but received indifference instead, this disparity could diminish your self-assurance in adulthood.

Signs that you may be encountering your shadow could include:
- A tendency to over-apologize

- Self-blame during adverse events
- Persistent feelings of guilt
- Disproportionate emotional reactions to daily stresses
- Irritability or impatience with minor annoyances
- Specific emotional triggers that seem inexplicable
- A habitual inclination to accommodate others, often at your own expense

These responses may stem from various childhood experiences, such as:

- Lack of emotional support or recognition
- Consistent undervaluing or neglect
- Discouragement from expressing personal talents or interests
- Exposure to family instability or significant changes
- Encounters with neglect or various forms of abuse
- Experiences of not meeting someone's expectations
- Absence of affectionate support like comfort or praise
- Taking on adult responsibilities prematurely

Consider the following scenario: A child is tasked with maintaining cleanliness in their living space, which involves routine chores such as cleaning their room or organizing play areas. Suppose this child occasionally neglects some of these duties, choosing to play instead. If a parent's response—while well-intentioned—feels overly critical to the child, it could evoke feelings of inadequacy or frustration. This scenario does not imply parental failure but highlights how subtle discrepancies in emotional support can shape a child's perception of acceptance and criticism.

Acknowledging the existence and influence of your shadow self is not about assigning blame but rather about deepening your understanding of how early experiences shape your emotional landscape. This awareness promotes a compassionate approach to self-healing, providing you with the tools to reconcile your inner and outer worlds for a more fulfilling life.

Reconnection With Your Inner Child

Every individual carries a piece of their childhood within them, reflected in their reactions, joys, and fears. This essence, known as the inner child, accompanies us through every stage of life, subtly shaping our actions and responses. Unresolved issues from our past, particularly those stemming from neglect—whether deliberate or circumstantial—cast shadows that persist.

Neglect is not always overt. Sometimes, it is the absence of nurturing during critical moments or the inconsistency in care that leaves lasting impressions on a child's psyche. These experiences manifest in two primary ways. First, the physical aspect, where basic needs like food and shelter are irregular, leads a child to feel insecure and undervalued. Second, the emotional aspect, where the absence of supportive, affirming interactions fails to cultivate a sense of safety and belonging.

Imagine the child who, instead of having a consistent presence to rely on, frequently finds themselves alone or overlooked. Envision a young mind yearning for affection and guidance, only to encounter emptiness or preoccupation. These are the moments that shape the shadows, the aspects of ourselves we learn to conceal or disregard.

However, our path to healing commences with acknowledging these shadows. It involves meeting that younger version of ourselves not with judgment, but with the curiosity and kindness of a newfound friend. Consider the simplicity with which children form connections, their openness, and immediate trust. That is the approach to adopt when reestablishing a connection with your inner child.

Engage in activities that ignite a child's world. Reconnect with the unbridled joy of splashing in puddles or the whimsical delight of singing loudly in an open field. Allow yourself to sketch freely on a blank canvas, letting shapes and colors flow without restraint.

Alternatively, immerse yourself in the vibrant pages of a coloring book, reveling in every stroke that ventures beyond the lines. As adults, we are often constrained by the need for control, constantly planning every moment and adhering to rigid schedules. However, embracing a childlike perspective entails learning to live in the present moment, and finding happiness in the spontaneous and the unplanned. Ask yourself: What truly brings me joy? What does it mean to live freely, even if only for a fleeting moment?

This reconnection is not about forsaking adult responsibilities but rather about blending the spontaneity and joy of childhood into our adult lives. It is about permitting ourselves to dance freely under the starlit sky, to break into song amid the hustle of daily commutes, or to sprint like the wind through open spaces, liberated from self-judgment. By nurturing this reconnection, we not only heal but also liberate ourselves to wholeheartedly embrace the vibrancy of life. Through the lens of the inner child, we discover wonder in every shadow and light in every corner, infusing each moment with boundless possibility and joy.

Recalling Your Earliest Memories

Reflect on the earliest memory you have of yourself as a child, or if no specific memory comes to mind, consider a cherished object such as a toy or blanket that you had before you turned five. Use this memory or object as a connection to your early childhood self.

Estimate the age of the child in your memory. Observe their facial expressions and body language. What might this child be thinking or feeling?

_____

_____

_____

_____

_____

_____

Reflect on your feelings toward this younger version of yourself. What words would you offer if this child were here with you today?

_____
_____
_____
_____
_____
_____
_____

Exploring a Childhood Moment

Picture yourself at a certain age during your childhood, choosing the first age that comes to mind.

How old are you in this memory? What about this particular age stands out to you? Look at the expressions and posture of this younger self. What might this child be experiencing in terms of thoughts and emotions?

_____
_____
_____
_____
_____
_____
_____

Consider your current feelings toward this version of yourself. If you could interact with this child today, what would you want to say? What does this child need from you? How could you meet these needs?

_____
_____
_____
_____

Reflecting on a Challenging Childhood Memory

Throughout a 17-year childhood, many experiences shape us. Think back to a challenging event from your childhood that you remember well. Use this exercise to delve into the details of that memory, but let your thoughts guide the exploration.

Describe the event. What occurred during this challenging time?

_____
_____
_____
_____

How did you feel when this event was happening?

_____
_____
_____
_____

Now, when you recall this event, what thoughts come to your mind? Are there any physical sensations that arise as you think about it?

_____
_____
_____
_____
_____

How has this event influenced your perceptions of yourself, others, and the world?

_____
_____
_____
_____
_____
_____

Consider the broader impact of this event on your subsequent childhood years. How did it affect your later experiences and development?

_____
_____
_____
_____
_____
_____

Supporting Your Inner Child

While we cannot change our past, we can mentally return to those moments and offer the support our inner child lacked during their hardest times. Think of an instance when you, as a child, needed but did not receive adequate adult support.

Visualize yourself as an adult witnessing this difficult moment for your younger self. How do you see this scene unfolding? How would you intervene or support your younger self as the adult you are today? What comforting words or actions would you offer?

Offer reassurance to your inner child that you are here now, ready to provide the care and protection they need.

_____
_____
_____
_____
_____
_____
_____
_____
_____
_____
_____
_____
_____
_____
_____
_____
_____

Exploring Betrayal

As children, we depend on our caregivers for security, safety, support, care, and love. Sometimes, however, those who are supposed to protect us end up betraying our trust.

Think about a time when someone close to you hurt or betrayed you. How did they betray your trust?

_____
_____
_____
_____

Reflect on whether you ever hold yourself responsible for their actions. It is important to recognize that their betrayal was not your fault.

_____
_____
_____
_____

Consider what would have been the right way for them to act in that situation.

_____
_____
_____
_____

Craft a statement that acknowledges and validates the feelings of your inner child about this betrayal, reaffirming that the fault was never theirs.

_____
_____

Writing a Letter to Yourself

Responsibility: *Embrace self-forgiveness by accepting responsibility for your actions. Acknowledge your mistakes directly without dwelling excessively on self-criticism or making excuses.*

_____
_____
_____
_____
_____

Remorse: *Reflect on how feelings of regret, guilt, and shame, though uncomfortable, can serve as catalysts for personal growth. Explore how past behaviors have adversely affected your present self.*

_____
_____
_____
_____
_____

Restoration: *Offer a sincere apology to yourself, specifying the behaviors for which you are seeking forgiveness. Outline actionable steps to correct these past errors and reconcile with your present self.*

_____
_____
_____
_____
_____
_____
_____
_____

Renewal: *Investigate the underlying reasons behind your regrettable actions. Devise strategies to address these root issues to prevent future occurrences. Consider what positive behaviors you can adopt moving forward and how you can use this experience as a stepping stone for personal development.*

_____
_____
_____
_____
_____
_____
_____
_____

Confronting the Inner Critic

In the left column, list three self-critical thoughts you have encountered recently. In the right column, write statements that counteract each of these critical thoughts, providing encouragement and support from your inner nurturer.

Inner Critic's Claim...	Inner Nurturer's Response...
"I always mess things up."	"Everyone makes mistakes. I learn and grow from each experience."

Inner Critic's Claim...	Inner Nurturer's Response...

What emotions or physical sensations do you experience when your inner critic speaks?

_____

_____

What emotions or physical sensations do you notice when your inner nurturer speaks?

_____

_____

Chapter 3:
Childhood Influence on Adult Life

Linda constantly felt she was teetering on the verge of a breakdown. Approaching her fifties, she frequently found herself on the verge of tears—an unsettling occurrence triggered by minor mishaps at the bakery or a sense of exclusion from a friend's online photo. While it might seem unusual for someone of her age to react with such intense emotion, Linda's responses were deeply rooted in her past.

During her discussions with a counselor, Linda disclosed feeling consistently overlooked, mirroring her experiences from childhood. Growing up as the youngest of five in a bustling household, Linda learned that only those who spoke the loudest received attention. This lesson continued to influence her adulthood in unproductive ways. She often felt insignificant and overlooked, as if her seven-year-old self was still trying to navigate a world that felt overwhelmingly vast and indifferent.

It is not uncommon for individuals to revert to childhood coping mechanisms during times of stress. Many people find that when they are under pressure, their reactions are disproportionate, echoing dynamics from their formative years. This tendency can manifest in various aspects of life, especially in relationships, where old wounds resurface, calling for acknowledgment and healing.

The challenge lies in recognizing these moments and understanding that they stem from our inner child seeking recognition and healing. It is essential to respond to these calls with compassion rather than frustration, acknowledging the impact of the past while striving to cultivate healthier responses.

If this resonates with you, take some time to reflect on instances when you react unexpectedly. Understanding the roots of these reactions can be the first step toward change. By addressing these deeply ingrained patterns, we not only enhance our interactions but also provide our inner child with the attention and care they require, paving the way for a more balanced and fulfilling life.

The Impact of Childhood on Relationships

Human connections are fundamental to our social existence, remaining as crucial today as they were in ancient times when survival hinged on strong communal bonds. Despite societal advancements, the dynamics of our early years continue to shape how we navigate relationships in adulthood.

Consider the phenomenon of oversharing: Encountering someone who immediately reveals intimate life details, from personal health issues to family conflicts, can be overwhelming. This behavior often originates from an unmet childhood need for attention, where being heard was the only way to feel seen. Similarly, individuals who struggle with setting or respecting boundaries likely grappled with similar issues during their formative years. In the absence of clear boundaries, relationships can become sources of discomfort and conflict.

Jealousy, too, is a relationship challenge often rooted in the inner child. It typically reflects deep-seated fears and insecurities that were inadequately addressed in childhood. Extreme jealousy has the potential to undermine trust and intimacy, transforming potentially healthy relationships into toxic ones.

Furthermore, remaining in unhealthy relationships can signify unresolved childhood trauma. People often persist in familiar—even painful—patterns because they mirror the relationships observed or experienced during upbringing. Recognizing these patterns is the initial step toward healing. Identifying when something feels amiss and consciously processing these emotions can empower individuals to break free from the cycles tethering them to past traumas.

The Impact of Childhood on Work

In professional environments, the echoes of our childhood selves often persist but can manifest differently. For instance, being extremely sensitive to criticism may signal an inner child that faced frequent discouragement or excessive criticism. This sensitivity can impede one's ability to embrace constructive feedback necessary for personal and professional development.

Similarly, the inclination to please everyone—to take on more tasks than manageable or to agree when one truly wants to decline—stems from a childhood desire for approval and acceptance. While traits like teamwork and dedication are commendable, sacrificing personal well-being for approval can lead to burnout and resentment.

Addressing these tendencies entails recognizing signs of overwhelm and allowing oneself the space to step back and assess personal needs versus professional demands. Establishing boundaries at work, as in personal relationships, is essential for safeguarding mental health and ensuring career satisfaction remains intact.

By acknowledging the influence of our inner child in both personal and professional spheres, we pave the way for more mature and gratifying interactions. This involves nurturing our inner selves while cultivating healthier, more sustainable relationships with others.

Embracing and Healing Your Inner Child

Healing your inner child is imperative because it embodies a fundamental aspect of your identity. Neglecting this facet is similar to disregarding a physical injury: both necessitate attention and nurturing for overall well-being. Tending to the wounds of your inner child goes beyond merely addressing past hurts—it is about unlocking a part of yourself that holds the key to your full potential.

As you confront your past wounds, you often unearth a concealed aspect of yourself, one that has been muted or overlooked but is indispensable for realizing your aspirations in life. The healing journey can be empowering, allowing you to regain mastery over your emotions and choices, and molding your life into one that mirrors your true aspirations.

Steps to Embrace and Heal Your Inner Child

Embarking on this journey requires dedication and patience, with each phase tailored to your unique experiences. Here is a roadmap to guide you through the healing process:

1. **Recognize the Inner Child:** This foundational step involves acknowledging the presence of your inner child and the memories it holds. This recognition is crucial as it sets the stage for healing.

2. **Affirm Your Experiences:** It is common to dismiss or downplay painful emotions and experiences. However, doing so can lead to those feelings manifesting in unhealthy behaviors or emotional patterns. Instead, confront and validate your past pains, acknowledging their impact on your life.

3. **Discover Unmet Needs:** Reflect on what you lacked during critical moments of your childhood—be it emotional support, physical safety, or encouragement. Understanding these deficiencies can help you provide for your inner child now.

4. **Offer Support to Yourself:** With a clear understanding of your needs, you can begin to nurture your inner child. Whether it is through self-affirmation, providing the comfort you were denied, or simply acknowledging your resilience, support yourself as you would a loved one.

5. **Prepare for the Future:** Use your newfound harmony with your inner child to handle future challenges. Visualize encountering similar situations and imagine yourself managing them with the strength and wisdom gained through healing.

Healing your inner child is an ongoing journey that thrives on consistent self-reflection. Engaging in activities like morning meditation, bedtime journaling, or regular self-check-ins helps maintain awareness of your inner state, which is crucial for sustained healing.

Following this structured approach not only supports personal growth but also enhances your interactions with others. A healed inner child leads to healthier relationships and a more fulfilling life.

Embracing Your True Self

It is profoundly unsettling when external voices—from media to societal norms—insist that you conform to an impossible ideal. This theme is powerfully echoed in the poignant monologue from the 2023 Barbie movie, which captures the relentless societal expectations placed especially on women.

In a scene that reflects both vulnerability and the harsh realities of these demands, Barbie grapples with an intense sense of inadequacy in a world dominated by unrealistic expectations. A human character in Barbie's seemingly perfect universe articulates the contradictions many women face: Be slim but not too slim, wealthy but never openly ambitious, assertive yet not aggressive, and perpetually youthful without appearing vain.

These mixed messages affect everyone, not just women; men also face their own societal pressures. The aim here is not to single out any particular group but to emphasize the unrealistic standards that society imposes on all individuals.

Self-acceptance is not about conforming to external expectations but about wholly embracing who you are, including areas that need improvement. Genuine self-acceptance involves acknowledging your flaws and accepting them as part of your identity while also committing to improving aspects of your life you wish to enhance.

For example, following a transformative self-improvement seminar, I began introducing myself in a way that emphasized my flaws: "Hi, I am Samantha, and I am overly sensitive and insecure." While this might seem like an act of self-acceptance, I soon realized it could hinder my personal growth by preemptively justifying my behavior.

Self-acceptance is not about using your nature as an excuse to remain stagnant. Instead, it involves acknowledging where you currently are while understanding that it does not dictate your future. It is about recognizing that you are more than your flaws; you have many commendable qualities that also deserve recognition.

Embracing your imperfections allows you to accept your humanity, complete with its messiness. Accepting that you are not perfect does not mean you are broken; it means you are authentic. This understanding is crucial because it forms the foundation for your journey of personal growth.

Self-acceptance also involves acknowledging your past, including any trauma and adverse experiences. Accepting these events is not about condoning what happened or excusing the actions of those who may have caused you harm. Rather, it is about confronting these experiences directly, no longer letting them lurk as hidden shadows in your life.

Acceptance is a powerful stance. It means facing your past and present honestly, and deciding for yourself the kind of future you want to create. In this sense, self-acceptance is both a beginning and an ongoing process that plays a crucial role in shaping a fulfilled and authentic life.

Journaling, a quiet dialogue with oneself, provides a sanctuary from the judgments of the external world. Each page serves as a canvas where every emotion, no matter how somber, finds expression. This simple practice is like whispering secrets into the wind—there is an inherent liberation in unveiling one's deepest thoughts and fears.

Imagine nurturing a tiny seed of improvement daily; its growth, though minuscule, accumulates astonishingly over time. Envision enhancing oneself little by little each day—how transformative that could be over a year! Let us explore some gentle yet powerful approaches to cultivating self-compassion and acceptance.

Begin your mornings by appreciating the small joys in life. Maybe today, it is the soothing rhythm of your breath or the early morning sunlight streaming through your window. Recognizing these simple pleasures can help you develop a broader appreciation for life's blessings.

When self-doubt becomes overwhelming, gently reshape its narrative. Transform "I cannot do anything right" into "I am learning from my experiences." This shift not only softens your inner dialogue but also empowers you to see yourself with compassion and potential.

Embracing daily forgiveness can significantly impact your self-perception. Forgiving yourself for a harsh word or a moment of envy may seem minor, but these small acts of forgiveness are essential for self-acceptance.

Some find morning reflections ideal for setting a positive tone for the day, while others prefer evening reflections to unwind and prepare for rest. Whatever time you choose, the consistency of this practice can lead to significant personal growth.

By acknowledging every part of yourself, even the less favorable aspects, you begin a healing process that encompasses your whole being. You assure your inner self of your commitment to growth and healing.

Through these practices, we learn not only to accept ourselves but also to embrace our journey with kindness and understanding. Each day offers a new beginning, a fresh page to write our story—one where we are the protagonist who, despite flaws and setbacks, moves forward with resilience and self-compassion.

Fear of Abandonment

Fear of abandonment is a common issue among those who have experienced abuse, neglect, or abandonment. This fear often encompasses a dread of the unknown, particularly concerning whether current relationships will eventually result in a withdrawal of support or protection. This anxiety can manifest in behaviors that unintentionally sabotage relationships, reinforcing negative self-beliefs such as, "People always leave me," or "I am not worthy of love."

In relationships, individuals with abandonment fears may display behaviors such as:

- Forming attachments quickly, often to partners who are unavailable or in relationships that are destined to fail
- Hesitating to fully commit, with a history of few long-term relationships
- Moving on swiftly from partners to avoid becoming too attached
- Staying in unhealthy relationships despite the personal toll
- Being overly critical and hard to please
- Struggling to trust others
- Overanalyzing situations and seeking hidden meanings

- Being extremely sensitive to criticism
- Having issues with needing to control situations
- Struggling to achieve emotional closeness

How do you experience or perceive fear of abandonment in your life?

_____
_____
_____
_____
_____
_____

Tracing the Roots of Fear

Explore the development of your fear of abandonment, beginning in infancy and progressing to the present. Identify the situations or relationships that intensified this fear throughout your life.

_____
_____
_____
_____
_____
_____
_____
_____
_____

Identify who abandoned you and in what way they abandoned you.

_____
_____
_____
_____

Reflect on the beliefs about people, yourself, and relationships that have developed as a result.

_____
_____
_____
_____

Consider whether you feel responsible for any instances of abandonment. Please explain.

_____
_____
_____
_____

What strategies do you employ to avoid feeling abandoned again? Do these behaviors inadvertently perpetuate the cycle of abandonment?

_____
_____
_____
_____

Reflecting on Abandonment

When we face abandonment, especially during childhood, it is common to internalize the blame, believing that our actions or inactions caused the loss. However, people often leave for reasons that are entirely unrelated to our behavior.

Delve into your own experiences with abandonment to identify instances where you might have wrongly blamed yourself. For example, you might have thought, "I believed my parents got divorced because I was poorly behaved," when in fact, "They got divorced due to irreconcilable differences that existed well before I was born." Examine these situations to understand the real reasons behind them and assess any self-blame you may have adopted.

_____
_____
_____
_____
_____
_____
_____
_____
_____
_____
_____
_____
_____
_____
_____
_____
_____
_____
_____

Analyzing Causes of Abandonment

Use this exercise to differentiate between self-focused and circumstance-focused causes of abandonment. Self-focused causes relate to personal attributes or behaviors you believe led to abandonment, while circumstance-focused causes involve external factors unrelated to your actions.

For instance, a self-focused cause might be, "They left because I was too clingy." In contrast, a circumstance-focused cause could be, "They left because they were building a career and did not have time to nurture a healthy relationship."

Explore and list the reasons under each category to better understand the dynamics behind your experiences of abandonment.

Self- Focused	*Circumstance-Focused*

Addressing Fear of Abandonment

What strategies can help me focus less on controlling future outcomes and more on the present moment?

_____
_____
_____
_____

In what ways might I be unintentionally undermining my relationships, and what proactive steps can I take to stop these behaviors?

_____
_____
_____
_____

Can I accept that people sometimes leave for reasons that have nothing to do with me, recognizing that their departure does not reflect my worth?

_____
_____
_____
_____

Craft two affirmations to remind yourself of your worthiness of stable, enduring relationships.

_____
_____
_____

Understanding Your Circle of Control

The fear of abandonment often originates from uncertainty, especially regarding the thoughts and intentions of others. While we cannot control external factors, we do have power over our perspectives, the energy we contribute, and our efforts within relationships. Redirecting attention toward what we can influence and releasing what we cannot is pivotal in handling the fear of abandonment.

Try this exercise to distinguish between the aspects of relationships that are within your sphere of influence and those that are not.

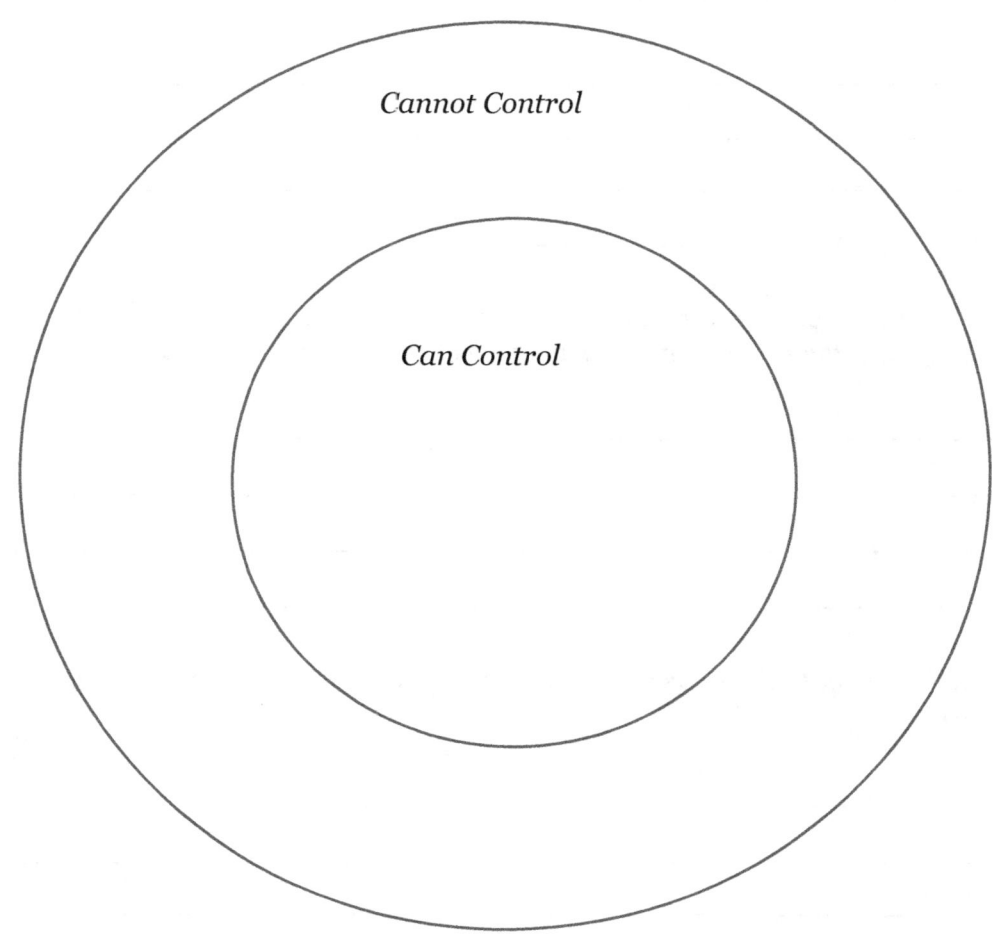

Abandonment Anxiety

Abandonment anxiety is often fueled by the fear that we are not equipped to handle someone leaving us, doubting our own resilience and capability to cope. It is vital to confront and challenge this misconception.

Describe a situation that triggers your anxiety or that you believe you cannot manage. For example: Going to a party and fearing I will not have anything to say.

_____
_____
_____
_____

Consider what actions you could take if your fear materializes. For example: I would engage others by asking about their interests, focusing on being an attentive listener.

_____
_____
_____
_____

Envision the worst-case scenario. For example: I end up not speaking to anyone all evening.

_____
_____
_____
_____

Reflect on how you would respond if the worst-case scenario occurred. For example: I would discuss the experience with someone I trust afterward and reassure myself that having a quieter night does not reflect negatively on my social abilities or self-worth.

_____

_____

_____

_____

Consider your responses and resilience in the face of losing a loved one or the end of a relationship. Reflect on your anticipated reactions and coping strategies. What do you envision happening if you were to lose a significant relationship? How would you respond to such a loss? What specific actions would you take to manage your feelings and situation? What coping mechanisms do you believe would help you through this time? Outline the steps you would take to ensure you continue moving forward in a healthy way.

_____

_____

_____

_____

_____

_____

_____

_____

_____

Transforming deeply ingrained beliefs and behaviors associated with the fear of abandonment demands patience, intentional action, and unwavering practice. Employ this exercise to strategize actionable steps for conquering these fears:

What practical steps can I implement today to alter my perspective on relationships?

_____

_____

_____

_____

What actions can I take today to ensure I am fully engaged and present in my relationships?

_____

_____

_____

_____

_____

What misconceptions about relationships and my own fears of abandonment do I need to start questioning? Can I fully accept that these beliefs might not be true? What proof can I gather to demonstrate that these beliefs are unfounded?

_____

_____

_____

_____

_____

Addressing Self-Abandonment

Self-abandonment manifests when we neglect our physical, emotional, social, or spiritual needs, leading to a disconnection from our authentic selves. This might entail prioritizing others' needs over our own, conforming excessively to external expectations, or losing sight of our personal identity. Furthermore, neglecting the needs of our inner child can intensify feelings of self-abandonment.

Reflect on how you might be neglecting your own needs. Are there aspects of your life where you are not being true to yourself?

_____
_____
_____

Consider how you might be ignoring the needs of your inner child. Are there emotional or supportive needs from your past that you have not yet addressed?

_____
_____
_____

Identify actions you can take to be more present and supportive of yourself. What regular practices can you incorporate into your routine to better nurture your own well-being?

_____
_____
_____

Think about specific ways you can better attend to your inner child. What activities or practices can help heal past wounds and provide the comfort and security your inner child needs?

_____
_____
_____

Reflecting on Caregiver Relationships

The ways my parents, caregivers, or older siblings made me feel were...

_____
_____
_____

I felt loved and understood most by...

_____
_____
_____

I felt unloved due to...

_____
_____
_____

The person from whom I most needed love was...

_____
_____
_____

It bothered me greatly when (insert person) did...

_____
_____
_____

Reflecting on Home Environment

Did you often find reasons to stay away from home, such as lingering with friends, visiting other kids' homes after school, or engaging in after-school activities?

_____
_____
_____

Did you ever feel ashamed, embarrassed, or hesitant about inviting friends over to your house? If so, why? If not, why not?

_____
_____
_____

Chapter 4:
Defining Your Personal Space

Saying "no" can serve as a vital act of self-defense. It is a simple term, yet it carries the weight of a complete statement, signaling a limit to what we are willing to tolerate or engage in. For many individuals, especially women, uttering this word can pose a challenge. It is often perceived not as an act of self-preservation but as a rejection of one's duties to others.

Let us delve into the concept of setting boundaries. A boundary essentially delineates where one's personal space and responsibilities start and end, separating them from those of others. Establishing personal boundaries is like drawing a line around our personal space, defining what we are willing to accept and what we are not. Without these boundaries, we can easily lose ourselves in the expectations and demands of others.

Boundaries can manifest physically, such as declining physical contact like hugs, or emotionally, such as opting out of a discussion when one is not emotionally prepared. They may also involve demanding respect in interactions, such as insisting on being addressed respectfully.

In contemporary times, numerous individuals encounter difficulties in setting, maintaining, and respecting these personal boundaries. This struggle mirrors a larger societal concern where the skill of setting boundaries is undervalued. Consequently, this oversight frequently results in uncomfortable or potentially hazardous encounters.

Take, for instance, property laws, meticulously crafted to delineate clear boundaries. Whether one is a property owner or a tenant, these regulations define the parameters of one's living space, encompassing everything from the precise dimensions of the land to the specific guidelines governing its utilization. Such legal frameworks play a crucial role in averting and resolving disputes concerning space and its usage. Yet, unlike property lines, personal boundaries are not always as straightforward to enforce. Allowing a neighbor occasional use of your yard or borrowing items might initially seem harmless, but it can blur the lines of what is acceptable, complicating boundary enforcement later on.

Setting firm and clear personal boundaries is paramount for both mental and physical well-being. It is not about being unkind or selfish; instead, it is about safeguarding oneself from potential harm and ensuring that interactions with others remain respectful and appropriate. These clear boundaries aid in navigating the social realm with greater comfort and confidence, minimizing misunderstandings and fostering mutual respect.

Physical Boundaries

When examining our relationships and interactions, it is vital to acknowledge the significance of establishing boundaries, particularly concerning our physical well-being. Each person has their own threshold for physical contact, whether it is a simple handshake, a pat on the back, or a warm embrace. Respecting these boundaries goes beyond mere social etiquette; it is a demonstration of respect for personal autonomy and emotional comfort.

Picture yourself at a large family gathering. In some families, it is customary to greet each other with affectionate hugs. However, for individuals who find such close physical contact overwhelming, these well-meaning greetings can induce stress. Now, envision a scenario where someone politely chooses to wave hello instead of engaging in a hug. Although seemingly minor, this small gesture allows them to maintain their comfort level without succumbing to the pressure of others' expectations.

From a young age, we often navigate social interactions with little guidance. For instance, as a child, you might have been ticklish and found being tickled during playful moments uncomfortable. Even though laughter might have masked your discomfort, expressing a preference for not being tickled becomes essential over time. Consider a scenario where you communicate to your spouse that tickling is off-limits. This assertion is not about ruining the fun but about establishing respect for personal physical boundaries.

Recognizing and respecting these boundaries is not solely an individual responsibility; it is a mutual respect that requires nurturing in all relationships. Engaging in open dialogues about what feels comfortable and what does not can foster deeper understanding and respect. It is not about creating distance but about cultivating a safe environment where every individual feels valued and respected.

Begin by reflecting on personal experiences where you felt your physical boundaries were disregarded. How did these instances make you feel? What would you prefer in similar situations in the future? It is natural if these reflections evoke mixed emotions or if the answers are not immediately clear. Understanding our physical boundaries is an ongoing journey that evolves alongside our relationships and experiences.

As we mature, we gain the wisdom to redefine these boundaries according to our evolving needs. If certain interactions become uncomfortable, it is entirely valid to adjust those boundaries to ensure they align with your personal comfort level.

By cultivating an awareness of our physical boundaries, we not only empower ourselves but also encourage others to acknowledge and respect these preferences. This mutual respect for personal space not only enhances our interactions but also fosters greater self-awareness and emotional well-being.

Emotional Boundaries

Imagine yourself at a lively party, where everyone seems to exude energy effortlessly—except you, feeling increasingly drained. Suddenly, you are cornered by someone whose every word seems to siphon more of your energy away. This is not mere coincidence; you have encountered what some call an "energy vampire." While the term may sound theatrical, it accurately describes individuals who leave us feeling emotionally depleted.

Encounters like these underscore the significance of establishing emotional boundaries. Think of emotional boundaries as personal guidelines dictating what and how much you are willing to share with others. These boundaries serve to conserve your emotional energy and promote peace of mind. Have you ever found yourself divulging too much information, perhaps in a moment of vulnerability? Later, you might regret oversharing, questioning your own judgment. It is a relatable scenario that underscores the importance of establishing clear boundaries.

At times, emotional reactions can be disproportionate—like crying over a minor setback at work or reacting angrily to trivial annoyances. These responses often signal porous boundaries, where your emotional reactions do not align with the situation's significance.

Developing strong, well-defined emotional boundaries may seem daunting, but it is essential for maintaining your emotional well-being. Start by reflecting on what you are comfortable sharing and with whom. Consider if there are situations where you tend to overshare or take on others' emotional burdens unnecessarily. Reflect on whether you frequently get entangled in others' conflicts or dramas.

Understanding and setting your emotional boundaries is not about shutting others out but about safeguarding your emotional health and balance. It is about recognizing when to share and when to prioritize your inner peace, ensuring that your emotional well-being remains intact across various social dynamics.

Time Boundaries

In the relentless rhythm of life, time slips away, leaving us with moments we cannot reclaim. Amid this constant motion, mastering the art of setting boundaries around our time becomes essential for preserving balance and respect—for ourselves and others.

Picture waking up each morning with a clear sense of how you want to spend your time. Maybe it is dedicating an hour to a morning run or carving out an evening for a beloved hobby. This deliberate allocation of time is not merely a habit; it is a powerful act of self-honor.

Consider Clara, who never lets a week pass without spending hours tending to her garden. It is her sanctuary—a place where she discovers peace and renewal. Then there is Martin, who meticulously arranges his schedule to ensure he never misses his children's school plays or soccer games. He is determined not to let his professional life encroach on these precious moments.

Disagreements over how time should be respected can strain relationships as well. Take Leo, for example, who consistently prioritized his own schedule over the needs of others, often leaving friends waiting. His approach to time sharply contrasted with his partner, who always made a concerted effort to respect agreed-upon appointment times.

Beyond punctuality, setting boundaries around our time entails recognizing and prioritizing what truly matters to us. It is about declining an unnecessary meeting if it clashes with your child's performance or turning down a social invitation to recharge after a demanding week.

Ask yourself:

- Do I carve out moments in my day to simply breathe and unwind?
- Am I frequently overwhelmed by scheduling more tasks than I can handle?
- How often do I engage in activities that truly bring me joy?
- Have I established clear boundaries between my professional and personal life?
- Am I able to confidently accept or decline invitations based on my priorities?
- How do I ensure I prioritize time for my physical well-being?
- What strategies do I use to manage my commitments and balance leisure activities effectively?

Financial Boundaries

The concept of boundaries extends well into the realm of our personal belongings and financial resources. This section explores how to establish and maintain clear limits around your possessions and money, which are often as integral to personal well-being as emotional boundaries.

Consider my personal practices regarding personal space and belongings. I have always been cautious about letting new people into my personal space. It takes a certain level of comfort and readiness before I invite someone into my home, especially a date. Similarly, I am selective about lending out my possessions, whether it is tools or my beloved Nintendo

Switch. The latter is strictly off-limits to everyone, including my kids, until I have had my fill of gaming.

Money is another area where boundaries can blur. Whether it is lending money to friends or family, sticking to a budget, or making thoughtful purchases, finances are a sensitive topic rooted in cultural and personal values. Lending or bartering can lead to misunderstandings or resentment if one party feels shortchanged.

Establishing boundaries around material possessions is not just about protecting the items themselves; it is also about preserving mental peace and ensuring relationships remain intact amid potential misunderstandings about possessions or finances.

Take Julia, for instance, who learned a tough lesson about financial boundaries in her relationship. When her partner's business started to struggle, he suggested using their excellent credit to secure personal loans to support the business. Eager to help, Julia agreed without hesitation. She opened multiple credit cards in one day, racking up a staggering $235,000 in credit, which she handed over to her partner. Initially, the business thrived with this financial infusion, but soon complications arose, and it became unsustainable. When the business failed, payments on the cards stopped, leaving Julia with a debt far beyond her means. Her partner suggested bankruptcy as the only solution, making Julia realize the depth of her misplaced trust. This financial disaster was not just about money—it highlighted violated boundaries and a lack of mutual respect. The aftermath was painful: They divorced, and Julia was left to manage the enormous debt on her own.

Julia's experience underscores a crucial lesson: Compromising your boundaries, especially financial ones, allows others to dictate the terms of your life. This can lead not only to financial ruin but also to emotional and psychological distress. Julia learned, as many of us must, the importance of establishing and maintaining clear personal boundaries. This was not just a financial lesson but a broader realization about self-respect and personal integrity.

This lesson extends beyond individual experiences to a universal truth. We all have limits where compromise may be too costly. Recognizing and defending these limits is not selfish; it is essential for self-preservation.

Take a moment to consider these prompts to gain insight into your boundaries regarding your belongings:

- *How comfortable am I with others using my belongings?* Reflect on your level of comfort with others using your possessions. Are you generally open to sharing, or do you prefer to keep your belongings private?

- *Are there specific people I prefer not to lend to?* Think about whether there are individuals to whom you hesitate to lend your belongings, and consider why you might feel this way. It could be due to past experiences or a gut feeling about their reliability.

- *Have I ever felt pressured to share something I own?* Recall instances where you may have felt pressured to share your belongings despite feeling uncomfortable. Consider how you responded and whether you were able to assert your boundaries effectively.

- *Recall a time I felt uneasy about lending or sharing an item.* Reflect on past situations where you felt uneasy about lending or sharing an item. What factors contributed to your discomfort, and how did you handle the situation?

- *Could saying "no" to someone about using my things potentially harm our relationship?* Consider whether saying "no" to someone about using your belongings could potentially strain your relationship with them. Reflect on how you navigate this balance between maintaining your boundaries and preserving your relationships.

While this list of boundaries is not comprehensive, it is a solid starting point. In both personal and professional relationships, knowing when to say "no" protects us from exploitation and harm. It empowers us to live on our own terms, make decisions that align with our values, and lead lives marked by self-respect and mutual respect.

Reflect on your boundaries today. Are they clear? Are they firm enough to protect you yet flexible enough to allow healthy relationships to flourish? Balancing this is challenging but crucial. Setting and respecting boundaries is not just about saying "no." It is about creating a life of integrity and mutual respect—a life where you are truly in control.

The Impact of Unclear Boundaries

Everyone has a friend like Jamie. She was vibrant, drawing attention in every room she entered. Her life was a series of spontaneous adventures, and she made sure you were along for the ride. However, the charm wore thin when her demands extended into my personal life, encroaching on my time and emotional energy. At first, Jamie's tendency to cross boundaries was subtle. She would call late at night, expecting long conversations about her latest crisis. Missing a call meant an onslaught of messages, each escalating in displeasure. At the time, it seemed easier to answer her calls than to address the real issue: my vanishing personal boundaries. The real wake-up call came during a difficult breakup when I needed support. Jamie was unavailable, wrapped up in her own world. This starkly highlighted how my boundaries with her had not just blurred; they had disappeared entirely.

This experience taught me the importance of establishing and maintaining boundaries. It is a common challenge in life, whether we face pushy friends, demanding jobs, or complicated family dynamics. We often begin with clear ideas of what we consider acceptable, but these boundaries can erode over time. When we fail to uphold our limits, others learn they can disregard them without consequence.

Take Robert, for instance. He always viewed himself as a committed employee. However, his readiness to stay late and take on additional projects gradually transformed his eight-hour workday into a relentless cycle of overtime and stress. His initial willingness to accept extra tasks set a precedent that he found difficult to change, ultimately leading to burnout.

Both stories highlight a crucial element of personal growth: the importance of understanding and asserting your boundaries. Recognizing when others encroach upon your space allows you to take action before you lose sight of your limits. It is not about erecting walls but about drawing lines that safeguard your well-being.

Setting boundaries is not merely a defensive act; it is a proactive one. It requires self-awareness to identify what you can handle and what drains your energy. It means being able to say "no" without guilt, knowing that doing so enables you to say "yes" to what genuinely matters.

For those who struggle with maintaining boundaries, start small. Focus on one area where your limits are being tested. Communicate your needs clearly and consistently. Remember, boundaries are not just about excluding others; they are about creating a space where your true self can thrive.

Inner Child and Boundaries

Our formative years significantly influence how we manage and set personal boundaries in adulthood. Imagine growing up in an environment where financial responsibility is either clearly demonstrated or barely mentioned. A child in a household where budgeting is as regular as breakfast is likely to become an adult with a strong understanding of financial limits. In contrast, a child in a home where money is a taboo topic may struggle to navigate their financial future.

Reflecting on my own childhood, my awareness of my family's financial situation was limited. I remember catching bits of budget discussions and occasionally hearing, "We cannot afford this month," which introduced me to the idea of budgeting. My parents allocated a modest allowance for themselves, using it sparingly or saving it for larger purchases. Despite these glimpses, the overall financial strategy remained a mystery to me.

Education provided the basics, like how to balance a checkbook, but did not cover the implications of debt or the importance of investing. This lack of comprehensive financial education left me with vague boundaries regarding money. As an adult venturing into independence, I had a confusing rule: Never spend more than you earn unless you can handle the credit card payments. This guideline was as unclear as it was unhelpful, leading to suboptimal financial decisions.

After graduating high school, I faced a harsh financial reality. I managed to stay afloat with two car payments and rent for a sparsely furnished apartment. My financial strategy was reactionary rather than proactive. I could keep up with my expenses, but I did not fully grasp the consequences of exceeding my financial limits until I faced them head-on. It is not just about the numbers; it is about understanding the boundaries those numbers represent. Money was more than a medium of exchange—it tested my personal discipline and reflected my self-imposed limits.

Reflecting on this, it is evident that the roots of our financial boundaries—or the lack thereof—are often planted in our childhood experiences. We observe and absorb the financial behaviors modeled by our caretakers, and these early experiences shape our financial boundaries as adults.

In this story of financial boundaries, formative influences can show up in several ways:

- **Conflict:** You may impose your financial needs on others, pushing the boundaries of what is reasonable because your internal gauge was never properly set.
- **Avoidance:** You might avoid financial planning or discussions, leading to irregular and impulsive spending.
- **Denial:** You may ignore increasing bills or overdue notices because you were never taught to address financial challenges directly.
- **Compliance:** You may follow financial advice without truly understanding it, or worse, take on debts due to the influence of a partner or family member because you were not taught to assert your own financial boundaries.

Each of these behaviors highlights a struggle with financial boundaries, stemming from the lessons—or lack thereof—learned in childhood. To develop healthy financial boundaries as an adult, it is often necessary to relearn or reinforce lessons that were unclear or absent during your formative years. This involves redefining your financial limits and recognizing that these boundaries are about more than just money—they are about self-respect and self-preservation. By doing so, you not only safeguard your financial health but also establish a framework for asserting and respecting boundaries in all aspects of life.

How to Set Healthy Boundaries

Navigating the intricate dynamics of personal relationships requires a deep understanding of both our own needs and the needs of those we interact with. It is like an ongoing dance, where the steps may vary, but the melody of mutual respect and self-awareness remains constant. One of the most delicate yet vital elements of this dance is the ability to clearly establish and uphold our personal boundaries.

Consider the story of a mother and her teenage son, a scenario familiar in the tapestry of family life. The mother, a warm and affectionate individual, finds solace and connection in physical embraces. However, her son values his personal space more distinctly and is less inclined toward such displays of affection. Previously, the mother might have insisted on hugs, driven by her own preference for affection, unintentionally crossing the invisible boundaries her son had set around his comfort zone.

Through self-reflection and a dedication to understanding her son's needs, the mother transformed her approach. She began offering hugs but learned to accept her son's response without judgment or disappointment. Sometimes he welcomed the embrace, other times he offered a brief hug, and occasionally, he declined altogether. This shift in their interactions went beyond respecting physical boundaries; it demonstrated a profound respect for her son's emotional comfort and space. The mother's newfound empathy and consideration became a valuable lesson she could impart to her son, teaching him not only to establish his own boundaries but also to appreciate and respect those set by others.

Creating and maintaining boundaries is not merely a defensive measure; it is a proactive step toward nurturing both personal well-being and that of others. It requires introspection and a candid evaluation of what we can tolerate and where we draw the line. For instance, someone may decide that punctuality is non-negotiable for them due to past experiences of stress and anxiety caused by others' delays, which they no longer wish to endure. By clearly communicating this boundary, they set a standard for how they expect to be treated and mitigate future frustrations.

The process of setting boundaries is highly individualized and can vary as much as the boundaries themselves. What remains crucial is the clarity with which these boundaries are communicated and the consistency with which they are enforced. Effective communication not only reinforces one's own boundaries but also facilitates understanding and respect for the boundaries of others.

Here is some guidance to assist you as you navigate the path of setting and maintaining boundaries:

- **Identify Your Priorities:** Start by identifying what truly matters to you. Begin with smaller boundaries, gradually progressing to more significant ones. By focusing on these initial boundaries, you will develop the habit and confidence needed to address more complex issues that could significantly impact your life.
- **Embrace Discomfort:** Setting boundaries can feel uncomfortable, especially if you are not used to asserting yourself. It is normal to experience feelings of guilt or awkwardness initially. However, remember that boundary-setting is a skill that improves with practice. Over time, the discomfort will lessen as you become more adept at advocating for yourself.
- **Prepare for Emotional Reactions:** When someone crosses your boundaries, it is natural to experience a range of emotions. Give yourself space to process these feelings. It is okay to take a moment to collect your thoughts before addressing the situation. However, addressing it promptly can help alleviate discomfort and reinforce your commitment to your boundaries.
- **Respect Others' Boundaries:** Mutual respect is key in any relationship. If you encounter someone with different boundaries, such as personal space preferences, it is important to honor their comfort level. When faced with differing boundaries, prioritize the more conservative preference to ensure respect and comfort for all parties involved.

Defining and Communicating Personal Boundaries

Recognizing that we cannot control others is fundamental to maintaining personal boundaries. It is essential to take ownership of our actions and how we communicate our limits to those around us. There are different ways to express boundaries, but only one method effectively respects both parties' autonomy.

Consider the difference between statements, orders, and genuine boundaries. For instance, stating, "I feel uncomfortable when you treat me this way," merely expresses your feelings without setting a boundary. Similarly, commanding, "You must treat me with respect," seeks to impose a rule on someone else's behavior, which may come across as controlling. In contrast, a genuine boundary is clearly stated with a consequence that is within your control. For example, "If you continue to disrespect me, I will remove myself from this situation." This type of communication demonstrates the action you will take if your boundary is crossed, highlighting your agency and the personal nature of the boundary.

Reflecting on my own experiences, I initially approached boundaries more as orders than true boundaries. For instance, I would say, "I will leave at this time," attempting to enforce punctuality. However, I shifted this to, "This is when I plan to leave; if you are not ready, I will proceed without you."

When introducing the concept of boundaries, it is essential to approach the conversation with calmness and empathy. Not everyone who crosses a boundary does so with ill intent, and giving them the benefit of the doubt can lead to more constructive discussions. Be clear and specific about what behaviors you will and will not tolerate, and if necessary, provide examples where boundaries were previously violated. This clarity helps others understand your expectations and enables them to decide whether they can respect your boundaries.

Confronting Discomfort

Setting boundaries is often an uncomfortable process, particularly when it involves close relationships. It requires us to articulate our feelings and assert our needs, which can lead to difficult conversations. However, despite the initial discomfort, setting boundaries can yield significant benefits for personal growth and relationship dynamics.

For instance, when I returned to college with a six-month-old child, I relied on my mother for support. I asked her to care for her grandson a couple of weekends each month. Initially, this arrangement went smoothly, fostering warm exchanges and shared parenting experiences. However, tensions arose when my mother began offering unsolicited and increasingly critical advice on my parenting. Comments like "Why would you let him cry like that?" or "You are ruining this kid" started to strain our relationship.

Initially, I brushed off these remarks as well-intentioned suggestions. I thought we simply needed time to adjust to our new roles—her as a grandmother and me as a mother. However, as the critical comments persisted, they began to take a toll on me. During a particularly stressful phone call about an upcoming visit, I reached a breaking point. I firmly expressed that her harsh judgment was unwelcome and that if it continued, it would force me to reconsider her involvement in our lives. This confrontation, while undoubtedly difficult, proved essential. It initiated a conversation involving my father as well, during which we collectively concluded that severing ties was not the solution. Instead, we opted for a compromise: My mother agreed to temper her criticisms, and I committed to seeking her advice only when necessary. This mutual boundary not only preserved our relationship but ultimately strengthened it.

Asserting your boundaries is vital. It clearly communicates to others what you consider unacceptable, allowing them to decide whether to respect your wishes. While confronting boundary violations can be intimidating, addressing them directly, even if they occur unintentionally, is crucial. People may not always recall or grasp new boundaries immediately, so open communication about any transgressions and your feelings toward them is essential.

Reflecting on this incident with my mother, which occurred nearly 14 years ago, I realize that navigating and respecting the boundaries we set required time and effort from both sides. However, the outcome has been immensely gratifying. Today, we share a robust, healthy relationship, and my son is thriving. It was through that challenging conversation that we discovered a path forward.

Unfortunately, not everyone will respect the boundaries we set. Some individuals may persistently disregard them, either due to their own boundary issues or a lack of respect for ours. In such cases, it is imperative to consistently address these violations. If someone continuously disrespects your boundaries despite discussions, it may be necessary to reassess their role in your life. It is entirely acceptable to distance yourself from those who persistently violate your boundaries to safeguard your well-being.

Boundary Exploration

The exercises that follow are tailored to guide you through the journey of recognizing your own boundaries, appreciating their importance, and acquiring practical methods to assert and communicate them effectively to others. Whether it involves establishing clear limits in personal relationships, upholding professional boundaries in the workplace, or reinforcing internal disciplines, these activities are crafted to provide you with the necessary tools and insights to assert your space confidently and enhance your well-being. Get ready to immerse yourself in the art of boundary setting—a crucial skill that will bolster your resilience, refine your interactions, and strengthen both your personal and professional life. As you engage with these exercises, you will gain clarity and assurance in your capacity to safeguard your energy and prioritize your needs.

What emotions or thoughts arise when you hear the word "boundaries?"

_____

_____

_____

_____

Reflect on your early lessons about boundaries. How were they taught or demonstrated in your upbringing?

_____
_____
_____

Identify what factors in relationships make you feel safe versus unsafe.

_____
_____
_____

Assess your comfort with declining requests. Can you say "no" without feeling guilty?

_____
_____
_____

Consider your ability to refuse without needing to explain.

_____
_____
_____

Think of a simple way you can begin practicing setting boundaries in your daily life.

_____
_____

Explore any fears that surface when you consider enforcing your boundaries.

_____
_____
_____

Determine which boundaries are crucial for your personal safety and well-being.

_____
_____
_____

Visualize what it would look like to firmly establish your boundaries.

_____
_____
_____

List the potential benefits of maintaining clear boundaries.

_____
_____
_____

Identify any obstacles that could hinder you from setting or maintaining your boundaries.

_____
_____
_____

Evaluate whether you truly believe you deserve to have your boundaries respected and upheld.

_____

_____

_____

Boundary Affirmations

- Prioritizing my well-being is essential.
- Setting boundaries is not an act of rudeness.
- My voice is important.
- Boundaries are an expression of self-love and self-respect.
- Healthy boundaries facilitate connection; they are not barriers.
- By establishing boundaries, I teach others how to treat me with respect.
- It is healthy and appropriate to set limits.
- I have the fundamental right to decline.
- My time and energy are precious and deserve protection.
- Communicating my needs is a form of self-care.
- I can establish boundaries without feeling guilty.
- I am entitled to choose my own availability, both emotionally and physically.
- Saying 'no' is a complete sentence and requires no justification.
- I honor my limits and trust that others will respect them.
- Prioritizing my peace does not mean I am selfish; it means I am self-aware.

Barriers to Setting Boundaries

Fear of rejection or abandonment	Fear of confrontation or causing displeasure
Feelings of guilt or shame	Uncertainty on how to establish boundaries

Reflect on which of these barriers resonate the most with you. Delve into their roots—do they originate from previous encounters, societal norms, or family influences? Investigating their origins can be instrumental in tackling and surmounting these hurdles. Contemplate seeking support and advice on boundary establishment from sources like literature, seminars, or therapy sessions to bolster your self-assurance and proficiency in this domain.

_____
_____
_____
_____
_____
_____
_____
_____
_____
_____

Setting Your Own Boundaries

The following exercise involves a structured template to help you articulate and set your boundaries effectively.

Boundary to be set:	
With whom/when?	
Why is it important?	
Statement I will use to set it:	

Boundary to be set:	
With whom/when?	
Why is it important?	
Statement I will use to set it:	

Boundary to be set:	
With whom/when?	
Why is it important?	
Statement I will use to set it:	

Boundary to be set:	
With whom/when?	
Why is it important?	
Statement I will use to set it:	

Boundary to be set:	
With whom/when?	
Why is it important?	
Statement I will use to set it:	

Boundary to be set:	
With whom/when?	
Why is it important?	
Statement I will use to set it:	

Boundary to be set:	
With whom/when?	
Why is it important?	
Statement I will use to set it:	

Boundary to be set:	
With whom/when?	
Why is it important?	
Statement I will use to set it:	

Boundary to be set:	
With whom/when?	
Why is it important?	
Statement I will use to set it:	

Boundary to be set:	
With whom/when?	
Why is it important?	
Statement I will use to set it:	

Boundary to be set:	
With whom/when?	
Why is it important?	
Statement I will use to set it:	

Setting Foundations for Strong Relationships

Before establishing meaningful and secure relationships, it is crucial to identify what you value most in your connections. What are your priorities? What are your non-negotiables? What matters less to you? Below is a list of potential relationship values. On the next page, rank your top five most important values. Feel free to add any values not listed that are significant to you.

Acceptance	Altruism	Compromise	Spontaneity
Fairness	Intimacy	Cooperation	Dependability
Well-Being	Personal Growth	Participation	Responsibility
Adventure	Health	Accomplishment	Security
Tradition	Connection	Freedom	Decisiveness
Loyalty	Inspiration	Helpfulness	Ease
Kindness	Persistence	Compassion	Integrity
Privacy	Open-Mindedness	Alignment	Honesty
Determination	Flexibility	Calm	Stability
Happiness	Fun	Peace	Consideration
Collaboration	Joy	Humility	Community
Celebration	Commitment	Affection	Friendship
Awareness	Balance	Appreciation	Safety
Sensitivity	Harmony	Support	Presence

Top 5 relationship values:

_____
_____
_____

Write each of your top relationship values into actionable behaviors. Describe what these values would look like in practice. For example, "We both actively contribute to the relationship by consistently showing effort, interest, and input to ensure its success."

_____
_____
_____
_____
_____
_____
_____
_____
_____
_____
_____
_____
_____
_____
_____
_____

I Am Worthy

I deserve relationships that are...	*I will stop blaming myself for...*
My boundaries in relationships include...	*My expectations in relationships are...*

Your Voice Matters

This section serves a unique purpose: It invites you to share your journey with others. While it may seem like a simple request to leave a review, your insights offer more than just feedback—they serve as a beacon for others who are still navigating their path to healing.

Impact Through Honesty

Your honest review can dramatically impact how others perceive their own journeys.

- **Support:** By sharing your experience, you offer others validation and understanding, which can be crucial for those who feel alone in their struggles.
- **Guidance:** Highlighting parts of the workbook that were particularly enlightening or challenging can direct others to the resources that might help them the most.
- **Inspiration:** Knowing that someone else has navigated similar challenges and found tools within these pages can inspire others to continue their pursuit of healing.

I urge you to take a moment to reflect on the changes you have noticed in yourself since beginning this workbook. What have you learned? How have you grown? Sharing these insights does not just help others; it reinforces your own journey and the steps you have taken toward healing.

Your voice is powerful and needed. By leaving a review, you do more than share your opinion; you extend a hand to those who are searching for the same peace and understanding. Thank you for being a vital part of this community and for contributing to a collective healing experience.

Scan to leave a review on Amazon if you live in the US

Scan to leave a review on Amazon if you live in the UK

Scan to leave a review on Amazon if you live in Canada

Scan to leave a review on Amazon if you live in Australia

Chapter 5:
Reparenting Your Inner Child

Imagine you are wandering through a dense forest, with each tree symbolizing a year of your life. Some paths are overgrown, and challenging to navigate due to the remnants of past struggles. Others are clearer, inviting a more effortless journey. This forest represents your inner world, and it is never too late to tend to the roots of your younger self and heal from past wounds. This inward journey, where you nurture yourself in ways you may not have been nurtured, transcends mere self-care; it is a profound act of transformation.

Consider yourself a gardener of your own soul. Perhaps your childhood lacked the exact nourishment you needed. Your caregivers, constrained by their own limitations and experiences, did their best. It was not out of malice. Life's garden is naturally wild and often overwhelming, making it easy for essential care to be overlooked.

Whether you have actively participated in parenting or merely observed from a distance, you possess the tools to start nurturing your own inner growth. This process involves revisiting the greenhouse of your past, not to fixate on the droughts or storms, but to water the soil anew and prune away the dead growth that no longer serves you.

First, let us rethink discipline—not as a strict rule or harsh rebuke, but as a gentle guide. It is about developing habits and rituals that enrich your life, teaching yourself with the patience and encouragement you needed as a child.

Next is self-care. Disregard the glossy images of indulgence that flood our screens. True self-care is foundational; it is the daily watering of our garden. This might mean nourishing your body with three wholesome meals a day, staying hydrated, or ensuring you get quality sleep. Sometimes, it is as simple as a solitary walk in the park or a quiet hour with a book.

Then there is the element of joy and wonder. Remember the exhilaration of childhood play? That sense of delight is still within you. Now, it might manifest in a creative project or the simple act of planning a small adventure on a weekend. It is about creating moments that ignite your innate curiosity and joy.

Lastly, emotional regulation is crucial. This involves learning to sit with your emotions, acknowledging them without letting them overwhelm you. Techniques like mindful breathing or journaling can help bridge the gap between chaos and calm, fostering harmony with your inner child.

By committing to this process, you are not just healing; you are thriving. You demonstrate to yourself, day by day, that you are worthy of care and attention. This is not about rewriting history, but about painting a new horizon—one where you stand tall, nurtured, and whole.

Nurturing Your Inner Child

As children, we absorbed behaviors like sponges. Whether it was emulating a parent's knack for organization, mimicking a teacher's thoughtful nod, or copying a friend's laugh, we learned by observing those around us. This instinct to adapt and adopt the nuances of our closest companions is a fascinating aspect of human nature.

Consider my friend Sarah, who unintentionally taught her toddler some colorful language due to her military background. One ordinary morning, driving her daughter to preschool, she was cut off by a hasty driver. Her immediate reaction was a sharp curse. Moments later, her daughter echoed the sentiment from her car seat, turning Sarah's frustration into a startled laugh. This humorous story highlights a deeper truth about influence and learning, particularly how we can guide our own growth as adults.

As we step into the role of nurturing our inner selves, it is crucial to be mindful of our internal dialogue. The stories we tell ourselves about our abilities—whether believing we are inherently bad at math or seeing ourselves as perpetual underachievers—shape our reality more than we might realize. Transforming these narratives through practices like journaling or affirmations can spark significant change.

Building self-confidence is another key aspect. Confidence is a skill honed through both trials and triumphs. Remember, each failure is not a stop sign but a guidepost, part of the journey to success. My own musical endeavors serve as a testament to this. Initially, my attempts at the violin were disastrous, leading me to believe that music was not for me. However, switching to the flute, encouraged by my supportive father, opened a new world of musical expression that I cherish to this day.

Effective communication is another essential skill for personal development. It is more than just constructing sentences; it is about ensuring our ideas are conveyed and understood as intended. Often, there is a gap between what we think we are communicating and what others perceive, leading to misunderstandings and frustration.

Ultimately, reparenting involves equipping your inner child with the skills and wisdom your adult self has gained. It is about revisiting those formative experiences with new resources and perspectives, fostering healing from the past and growth for the future. This self-guided journey is not just about healing—it is about thriving with a renewed sense of understanding and self-compassion.

Speaking to Your Inner Child

Everyone carries a part of their younger self within them, brimming with dreams and sometimes harboring silent whispers of past hurts. This inner child echoes through our laughter and lurks in our shadows, shaping who we are today. Nurturing this part of our psyche is not just an act of healing; it is a bold declaration of self-love and acceptance.

Imagine a child, vibrant and full of life, seeking affirmation in every little achievement, from the smallest drawing pinned on the fridge to a report card filled with top grades. This child, perhaps a reflection of your own past, believed affection and approval were prizes to be earned. If this belief was never corrected by the adults meant to offer unconditional support, the scar of conditional love might have woven its way through the fabric of their adult existence, affecting self-esteem and personal relationships.

Consider now the missed moments—simple joys like sharing a meal or playing catch—that could have anchored a sense of worthiness. Without these moments, one might carry a lingering feeling of being perpetually sidelined, even into adulthood. It is within these reflections that the journey of reparenting begins, rewriting the subtle scripts that have played in the background of your life.

Each morning, as you stand before your reflection, engage in a new ritual. Speak kindness to yourself with affirmations that resonate deeper than mere words: "I am cherished," and "I am deserving of good." Let these phrases be your mantra as you lock eyes with yourself, affirming your inherent worth.

This journey is not always illuminated; it often takes you through darker moments as well. Navigating these challenging parts of your story may necessitate the support of a compassionate professional. Seeking help is perfectly okay, as some aspects of healing are not meant to be faced alone.

Throughout this process, it is vital to celebrate the resilience of your younger self—the part of you that endured every difficult day. Show gratitude for their strength and recognize that every obstacle was overcome using the best resources available at the time.

As grown-ups, we hold within us the ability to heal and bring closure to the tales that began in our childhood. We possess the wisdom, resilience, and capacity for love that our younger selves yearned for. Taking the first step by apologizing to oneself or acknowledging that the mistakes of the past were not our own can spark a profound transformation. It marks a significant moment of reclaiming control over our own story.

Consider this an invitation not only to mend but to thrive, armed with a deep understanding of your history and a hopeful outlook on what lies ahead. Reconnecting with your inner child initiates a powerful journey that enables you to embrace and nurture every facet of your being. It is about assuming the role of guardian over your own happiness and crafting the blueprint for your emotional well-being.

Gardening the Self

Embarking on a journey of personal transformation is like entering a vast garden, where the paths ahead beckon with both challenge and beauty. It is a voyage that demands a delicate balance of determination and compassion, where every step offers an opportunity to nurture and evolve. Within this metaphorical garden, you are both the gardener and the blooming flower, tending to the wounds of the past while sowing the seeds of new aspirations.

Imagine this garden as a reflection of your mind, where each seed represents a pledge to yourself. Consider the simplicity of committing to a brief daily walk or a moment of mindfulness. Though seemingly small, these promises have the potential to yield significant growth over time. As you honor these commitments, the seeds of intention blossom into resilient plants, symbolizing the trust you have cultivated within yourself and the fulfillment of your aspirations.

In this garden of your inner world, every emotion is like the weather—unpredictable, fleeting, yet crucial for nurturing growth. We have all experienced the sting of having our feelings dismissed as too intense or insufficient. However, within the sanctuary of your personal garden, every raindrop and sunbeam holds significance, enriching the soil of your inner landscape. Rather than categorizing these emotional fluctuations as positive or negative, it is about embracing them as integral parts of your journey, responding with a heart attuned to equilibrium and resilience.

And amid this ever-changing climate, joy emerges as the unexpected bloom—a wildflower that blooms in the unlikeliest of places. It serves as a reminder that even amid the challenges of healing, moments of pure delight can be discovered in laughter, in letting go, and in the uninhibited dances performed when no eyes are watching.

Tending to this garden requires more than occasional care; it necessitates consistent nurturing, from uprooting weeds to safeguarding the most delicate sprouts. Similar to the deep-rooted coping mechanisms of our past, changing ingrained behaviors can be a lifelong endeavor. However, through steadfast dedication to this inner garden, new habits can take root and flourish, gradually transforming the landscape with each passing day.

Always remember, this journey is all about you—about embracing the person you were always meant to become. It is a voyage of self-discovery and self-care, where you learn to establish boundaries and nourish your soul with what truly sustains it, whether that is wholesome nourishment, supportive connections, or moments of serene solitude.

And when you witness the fruits of your labor, take the time to celebrate. Every small stride forward in this inner garden of self is a triumph worthy of acknowledgment. Whether it is the blossoming of a flower or simply the emergence of a new leaf, each represents your bravery and dedication to this journey of personal growth.

As you navigate through your garden, remember that every gardener's path is unique. Your journey unfolds at its own pace, presenting its distinct set of obstacles and victories. Embrace this process with the same tenderness and patience you would extend to any living thing, knowing that with time, your garden will reflect the beauty of your nurturing efforts.

Managing Life's Expectations

Think of the journey to adulthood as a path littered with numerous lessons that sculpt our identity—from the academic challenges of mastering literacy to the nuanced social nuances dictating attire for various occasions. These rites of passage are not mere milestones; they carry an unspoken burden of anticipation, each adding a bit more weight to our shoulders.

Imagine yourself as a budding artist navigating the complexities of painting. Initially, it is about understanding the differences between watercolors and acrylics. However, as you mature, each brushstroke is not just about artistry; it is also measured against the shifting expectations of mentors and peers. Their praise for a vivid sunset or a perfectly chosen hue for a tranquil sea sets a standard. While validating, it also subtly elevates the bar, transforming what was once a joyful expression into a potential arena of performance pressure.

Maybe you have experienced a moment at an art exhibition where the chatter of the crowd suddenly makes your hands shake, the brushes feel cumbersome, and the colors less forgiving. You might catch yourself making excuses about the lighting or the color mix—anything to avoid confronting that internalized fear of falling short of expected standards.

This sensation of being under scrutiny does not vanish with childhood; it embeds itself subtly in our psyche, even in adult endeavors. Simple tasks like writing, particularly personal reflections as found in this book, can feel intimidating. As I drafted chapters on personal challenges, every word seemed burdened by both past experiences and the anticipation of judgment.

To those grappling with similar pressures, I offer this advice: Be kind to yourself. When external or self-imposed expectations threaten to dictate your worth or progress, allow yourself to pause. Take a deep breath, sip some water, and perhaps step outside for a moment of fresh air. Remember, it is perfectly acceptable to move forward at your own pace.

Our value is not determined by how closely we adhere to external standards, but by how genuinely we navigate our individual journey. Offering ourselves compassion and understanding can free us from the weighty burden of anticipation, enabling us to fully embrace our authentic selves.

Reparenting Your Inner Child

Reparenting involves shedding harmful beliefs or behaviors acquired during childhood and fully nurturing your inner child. Here are four steps to guide you through the reparenting process:

1. **Acknowledge Your Inner Child:** Recognize the presence of your inner child and understand their needs.
2. **Affirm and Validate:** Support and validate your inner child's thoughts, feelings, emotions, dreams, wishes, and worries.
3. **Make Authentic Decisions:** Make choices that align with your true self rather than conforming to others' expectations.
4. **Reconnect With Play:** Engage in play, allowing your inner child to explore the world in a safe and supportive environment that you create.

From the steps outlined above, which one do you find the most challenging to implement? Why? Which step do you feel most prepared to take on? Why?

_____
_____
_____
_____
_____
_____

How can I work to acknowledge my inner child and their needs?

_____

_____

_____

_____

_____

How can I affirm and validate my inner child's thoughts, feelings, and emotions?

_____

_____

_____

_____

_____

How can I make decisions that are more authentically my own?

_____

_____

_____

_____

_____

How can I get back in touch with play?

_____

_____

_____

_____

_____

Addressing Unmet Childhood Needs

In the left column, list any needs you had as a child that were not met. In the right column, detail how you can fulfill these needs for yourself now as an adult.

My inner child's needs	I can meet this need by

Reparenting Affirmations

Read these affirmations aloud to nurture and reassure your inner child, helping them feel acknowledged and secure.

- *I cherish who you are and I am always here to support you.*
- *Making mistakes is perfectly okay and safe; every experience brings strength, clarity, and insight.*
- *I can now care for you in the ways you always needed.*
- *Your worth is inherent and does not depend on your achievements.*
- *I am incredibly proud of you.*
- *My love and affection for you are unconditional; perfection is not required.*
- *You have the right to express your needs and to seek assistance; you deserve to have your needs met.*
- *You have the freedom to define yourself; your unique self is precious.*
- *All your emotions are valid and welcomed; expressing them is healthy.*

Now, try creating some reparenting affirmations of your own...

_____
_____
_____
_____
_____
_____
_____

Overcoming Self-Judgment

At times, we may harshly judge ourselves for past coping mechanisms. This exercise is designed to help you replace self-judgment, shame, or embarrassment with self-compassion.

Judgment	Self-Compassion

Empowering Adult Commitments

As children, our control over our environments and reactions is often limited. As adults, we have the opportunity to assert control and set personal commitments to shape the life we aspire to live.

Consider drafting a list of commitments to guide your actions and behaviors.

I am going to...	*I am NOT going to...*
Examples: • Be honest with myself • Maintain a gratitude journal • Engage in a creative activity each week to connect with my inner child	Examples: • Yell at others • Indulge in negative self-talk • Resort to unhealthy coping mechanisms to avoid facing my true feelings

Exploring Myself

This exercise is designed to boost self-awareness and self-esteem.

Things I am good at:	*Things I do for others:*
Compliments I have recently received:	*Goals I have successfully achieved:*
Challenges I have successfully overcome:	*Things I appreciate about myself:*

Chapter 6:
Emotions and Childhood

Reflect on your childhood. Do you remember feeling overwhelmed by emotions you could not describe? Imagine a young child experiencing intense sadness or anger without the means to express it. Many adults find it difficult to recall their emotions from early childhood, with clear memories often not forming until around age eight or nine.

As children, we experience a wide range of emotions, from joy to fear, often lacking the vocabulary or understanding to articulate them. These feelings begin with basic emotions like happiness, sadness, anger, fear, and loneliness. As we grow, they become more complex, including emotions like guilt, love, and surprise. Without the ability to express these feelings, frustration can build up, leading to emotional wounds. If left unaddressed, these wounds can persist into adulthood, manifesting as lingering fears, anxiety, or shame.

The deep emotions we experience in childhood continue to influence us, often in ways we may not fully understand. Even if the specific events that triggered these feelings are forgotten, the emotions themselves are embedded in our physical and emotional being. These early emotional experiences have a significant and lasting impact, shaping our behavior and emotional health well into adulthood.

It is crucial to realize that these emotional imprints are not just remnants of the past; they actively shape who we are today. By understanding and addressing these hidden emotions, we can embark on a journey of healing and emotional growth. This process is not merely about recalling past events, but about recognizing their ongoing influence and learning new, constructive ways to deal with our emotions.

Understanding emotions is like unraveling a complex system where each part plays a vital role in shaping our responses to life's events. Here are five distinct stages, each uniquely contributing to our emotional experience.

1. **Initiation by an Incident:** Every emotional experience starts with a specific incident, which initially holds no emotional value. Imagine encountering something completely unfamiliar, like a "Skyglem Turner"—a term I have just invented. With no prior emotional reference, your interaction with this new concept is purely factual and free of bias.

   Whether the event involves routine activities like tying your shoes or significant occasions like a family dinner, these are merely factual occurrences. They remain emotionally neutral until we begin to process them further.

2. **Perception Through Personal Filters:** When an event occurs, our minds immediately start processing it through filters shaped by our personal history and senses. This filtering mechanism, a primitive survival tool refined over millennia, helps us interpret our surroundings.

   Consider the smell of a new car as an example. Initially, the scent of fresh leather is distinctive, but it soon fades as your brain deems it non-essential information. Our mental filters constantly prioritize and deprioritize information based on perceived relevance. These filters also create expectations based on past experiences, leading to selective attention. For instance, if you believe you are often unlucky with traffic lights, you will be more likely to notice every time you hit a red light, reinforcing your belief.

3. **Creation of Subjective Realities:** After being filtered, the objective event transforms into your subjective interpretation. This subjective reality is what truly influences your emotional response.

   For example, a simple question from your mother during coffee can trigger a range of emotional reactions based on the history and dynamics of your relationship. Your interpretation of her question is influenced by these past interactions, shaping your emotional reaction accordingly.

4. **Physical Manifestations of Emotions:** Emotions are not solely confined to mental states; they also manifest physically within our bodies. These bodily

responses occur automatically, regulated by our autonomic nervous system, which oversees our survival instincts, such as the fight-or-flight response.

Experiencing joy may result in relaxation, whereas anger can trigger an adrenaline rush, preparing you for action. These physiological reactions are universal and play a crucial role in how we navigate both threats and pleasures in life.

5. **Expression of Emotional States:** Emotions find their outlet through our behaviors. This phase is outwardly apparent and encompasses actions such as smiling, crying, clenching fists, or even shouting. These expressions serve as our means of conveying our emotional state to the world.

Each of these stages represents a progression in the emotional journey, from a neutral event to a fully articulated emotional expression. Grasping these stages aids us in gaining a deeper understanding of and effectively managing our emotional lives.

Identifying and Controlling Emotions

Have you ever taken a moment to acknowledge the whirlwind of emotions stirring within you? Pause for a moment—how do you feel at this very instant? Are you calm, anxious, joyful, or perhaps experiencing a subtler emotion? Identifying these feelings may appear straightforward, yet it unveils a vast emotional landscape far beyond the simple realms of happiness, sadness, or anger.

Visualize yourself at an amusement park. You find yourself in front of the intimidating roller coaster that has always filled you with dread. Your heart races, your palms become clammy, but instead of turning away, you confront your fear head-on. You admit to yourself, "I feel scared yet excited." This seemingly small act of recognizing your fear achieves something remarkable—it diminishes the hold that fear has over you.

A team of researchers from a prominent university conducted a captivating experiment involving individuals with arachnophobia or fear of spiders. They assembled these individuals and tasked them with approaching a tarantula as closely as they could. The participants were divided into groups and given varying instructions on how to confront their fear. One group was encouraged to vocalize their emotions, articulating statements like, "I am afraid of this spider." Another group used neutral language, while a third group was instructed to divert their attention by discussing unrelated topics.

A week later, the same individuals were invited to approach the tarantula once more. The outcomes were striking. Those who had verbalized their fear were able to approach the spider more closely with reduced distress and fewer physical manifestations of fear, such as sweaty palms, compared to the other groups.

This study highlights a potent tool within our reach: the capacity to label our emotions and, in doing so, exert some degree of influence over them. This does not imply immunity to emotional impact; rather, it empowers us to acknowledge that our emotions constitute only a portion of our overall experience, not the entirety of our being.

So, where does one begin with this practice? It is quite straightforward. Start by pinpointing what you are feeling at any given moment. Are you feeling stressed at work? Anxious about a social event? Take a moment to recognize and label these emotions. This marks the initial step toward developing emotional flexibility and transforming what can often feel like a turbulent journey into a more manageable one.

This approach does not demand drastic alterations; it commences with small recognitions. Through this process, you can begin to discern patterns in your emotional reactions and gain deeper insights into yourself. This self-awareness is pivotal not only for regulating your emotions but also for enhancing your overall life experiences, enabling you to confront fears and uncertainties with newfound clarity and assurance.

The importance of mastering your emotions is indisputable in a world where we all seek a sense of equilibrium. Recall the last instance when you felt overwhelmed by your emotions—likely, it was during a high-stress situation that made clear thinking nearly impossible. Everyone engages in emotional regulation to some extent, even if they are not consciously aware of it.

Imagine you are gearing up for a crucial presentation, but anxiety starts creeping in. Instead of letting panic take over, you opt for some calming music to steady your nerves. This seemingly small choice exemplifies emotional regulation. Similarly, picture moments when anger threatens to cloud your judgment. Instead of reacting impulsively, you pause, take deep breaths, or count to ten, granting yourself a chance to reassess the situation.

At the heart of emotional control lies the ability to create a space between our feelings and our actions. By managing our emotions, we steer clear of rash decisions driven by the intensity of the moment. Take Sarah's situation, for instance. In a fit of anger, she abruptly ended a long-term friendship over a misunderstanding about shared responsibilities in their apartment. Her impulsive actions left behind unresolved issues and severed connections. If she had taken a moment to regulate her emotions, perhaps a conversation could have salvaged their friendship.

This does not mean suppressing emotions; rather, it is about acknowledging them while preventing them from dictating our actions. It is about allowing ourselves to feel emotions while still making choices that serve our best interests.

Emotional Intelligence

Emotional intelligence is essentially the capacity to perceive, impact, and evaluate not only our own emotions but also those of people in our environment. This skill enriches our social interactions, deepening our comprehension of social subtleties and our self-awareness, thus facilitating the navigation of social intricacies. Importantly, emotional intelligence forms the foundation of effective interpersonal relationships, enabling us to respond empathetically and perceptively as we interact with others. It empowers us to react appropriately in emotionally charged circumstances or when individuals are visibly distressed, allowing us to maintain composure and prevent situations from escalating beyond our control.

- **Fostering Self-Awareness:** The journey toward emotional maturity commences with self-awareness. This entails consciously acknowledging one's feelings, motives, aspirations, and character. Self-awareness involves comprehending how our emotions and behaviors are perceived by others and whether they align with our personal standards. It necessitates a candid evaluation of our emotional state and the impact of our actions on those around us. Self-awareness is vital not only for self-reflection but also for effectively managing interpersonal connections. At times, individuals may recognize how they are perceived but opt to disregard opportunities for personal development, using their self-awareness as a shield against change or as a rationale for ingrained behaviors.

- **Mastering Self-Regulation:** Let us delve into the story of someone I worked with, whom we will refer to as Mark. Mark habitually dismissed any suggestions or requests, regardless of their nature. Whether it was a lunch invitation or a minor alteration in a work project, his response was always "no." This reflexive resistance stemmed from a profound fear of change, indicative of a larger underlying issue. Although Mark acknowledged his fear, he struggled to effectively regulate his emotional responses. Genuine emotional intelligence surpasses mere awareness; it entails actively managing one's emotions to promote both personal well-being and professional development. Imagine the potential transformations within our workplace if Mark could temporarily set aside his fears to objectively address his concerns. Such a shift could facilitate innovative problem-solving and more adept management of workplace challenges. Emotional intelligence necessitates not only the recognition but also the appropriate expression of emotions, ensuring they are conveyed at opportune times and settings. This might involve choosing to contemplate privately rather than reacting impulsively in public contexts.

- **Harnessing Motivation Through Emotional Clarity:** At the core of emotional intelligence lies a crucial understanding of who you aspire to be and the reasons behind those aspirations. Without a clear vision of your ideal self, navigating your emotional responses can pose a significant challenge. It is vital to dedicate time to envisioning the best version of yourself, infusing this vision with your deepest aspirations, dreams, and motivations. This exercise is not merely wishful thinking; it lays the groundwork for emotional evolution by aligning your current self with your future aspirations.

From childhood onward, our dreams shape our ambitions—whether they involve aspiring to become astronauts, presidents, or artists, these aspirations guide our paths of growth. However, as we mature, these aspirations often dim. Emotional intelligence encourages us to revisit and refine these dreams, offering a clearer perspective on the person we aim to become. Imagining your future self in vivid detail—how you navigate stress, respond to challenges, and carry yourself in everyday situations—helps solidify your emotional goals and personal development trajectory.

- **Crafting a Personal Vision and Understanding Your "Why":** Building on this vision requires more than just vivid imagination; it entails comprehending the motivations behind these aspirations. Pinpointing your "why"—the driving forces propelling you toward these personal transformations—is essential for maintaining motivation, particularly during tough times. This understanding acts as a compass, aiding you in navigating emotional dilemmas and harmonizing your reactions with your overarching objectives. For instance, if your vision encompasses prioritizing health, then opting for activities that channel your emotions constructively, such as exercise, becomes integral to managing your emotional well-being.

- **Reflective Practices for Emotional Maturity:** As we progress in our emotional development, we frequently engage in introspection regarding our responses and the stimuli prompting them. This reflective approach is indispensable, redirecting our inquiries from defensive "why" queries that can provoke defensiveness to more constructive "what" inquiries aimed at comprehension. For instance, rather than thinking, "Why did I respond so intensely?" you might ask, "What specific aspect of this situation elicited my reaction?" This shift not only aids in personal evaluation but also enhances interpersonal connections, fostering less confrontational and more enlightening interactions

- **Empathy: The Foundation of Emotional Intelligence:** At its apex, emotional intelligence culminates in empathy—the capacity to comprehend and resonate with others' emotions without assimilating them as our own. Empathy empowers us to perceive the world through another person's eyes, nurturing genuine connections and deeper insight. For example, when confronted with a child's emotional outburst, acknowledging their feelings and collaboratively exploring solutions can metamorphose potential conflict into a moment of bonding and mutual comprehension. Empathy is indispensable not only in personal relationships but also in professional settings, where appreciating diverse viewpoints can enhance teamwork and foster more harmonious interactions. It entails providing a haven for emotions devoid of judgment, facilitating a genuine grasp of underlying concerns.

Navigating Emotions

What emotions do you find yourself typically avoiding?

_____

_____

_____

As a child, which emotions were discouraged or deemed unacceptable?

_____

_____

_____

What concerns arise about feeling and expressing these emotions now?

_____

_____

_____

Imagine embracing these emotions. How could you start to accept them?

_____

_____

_____

Revisiting Childhood Beliefs

Our beliefs about ourselves and the world are shaped by early influences, including caregivers and childhood experiences. Trauma during these years can result in low self-worth, a negative outlook, and isolation.

Use this exercise to address and reassess any harmful beliefs from your childhood.

1. Identify a negative belief you have about yourself, others, or the world.	2. Reflect on the childhood experiences that contributed to the formation of this belief.
3. Identify what situations or events in adulthood trigger this belief.	4. Consider how this belief affects your day-to-day life now.
5. Evaluate whether there is any factual basis for this belief. What evidence supports it?	6. Think of alternative evidence, explanations, or thoughts that could counter or disprove this belief.

Reflecting on Your Childhood Home

Think back to the home where you grew up. Would you describe it as mostly stable or unstable? Consider if there was yelling, fighting, or abuse. Did you feel ignored, unloved, or unsafe at times? Reflect on the positives as well. Did you feel a sense of trust with those you lived with? Use this space to jot down all thoughts and memories that surface when you think of your childhood home.

_____

_____

_____

_____

_____

_____

Exploring Safe Spaces

If your childhood home did not feel secure, reflect on the places where you did feel safe. These could be actual locations or imaginary refuges you created during tough times. Answer the following to better understand these sanctuaries:

What were these safe places, and what aspects made them feel secure?

_____

_____

_____

_____

Describe the sensory details of these places: their appearance, scents, textures, and sounds.

_____
_____
_____

Was anyone with you in these places, or were you typically alone?

_____
_____
_____

How frequently did you visit or think about these safe spaces?

_____
_____
_____

Did others know about these places, or were they private retreats?

_____
_____
_____

Identify any common features or feelings these safe spaces shared.

_____
_____
_____

Growing Up Too Soon

Childhood trauma can accelerate maturity, often pushing children into roles and responsibilities meant for adults as they navigate significant emotional pain and complexity.

Reflect on the ways you had to act "grown-up" during your childhood.

_____
_____

Were you burdened with responsibilities or expectations that were too advanced for your age? What fundamental beliefs developed from these experiences?

_____
_____
_____

Did you find yourself in reversed roles, such as caring for your caregiver or assuming a parental role for your siblings?

_____
_____
_____

Consider the aspects or freedoms of childhood you feel you were deprived of.

_____
_____
_____

Exploring Maladaptive Behaviors

Reflect on the behaviors that have been shaped by your childhood experiences but are no longer serving you well. This exercise will help you understand the origins of these behaviors and consider healthier alternatives.

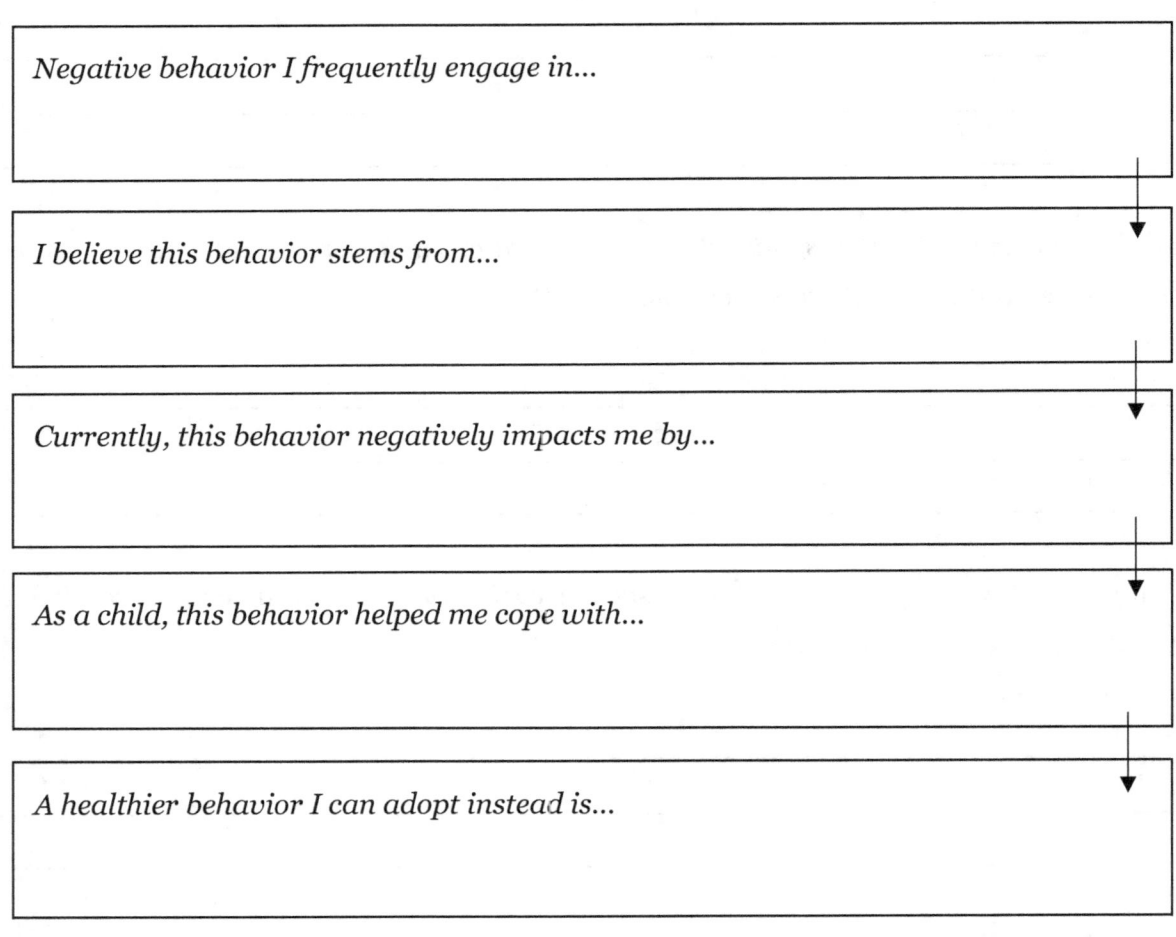

Negative behavior I frequently engage in...

I believe this behavior stems from...

Currently, this behavior negatively impacts me by...

As a child, this behavior helped me cope with...

A healthier behavior I can adopt instead is...

Express gratitude with a statement acknowledging your inner child's resilience. Also, affirm your commitment to change with a statement of intent to let go of this unhelpful behavior.

Chapter 7:
From Surviving to Thriving

Imagine setting off on a journey of self-discovery, where the path to your future is shaped not by destiny, but by your own aspirations. Visualize yourself as an artist, with your life as a blank canvas. What would you create? Perhaps you have felt adrift, simply reacting to life's circumstances without pausing to ask, "Is this truly what I want?"

There was a period in my life when every choice seemed predetermined. Friends would ask me, "What is your dream job?" or "Where do you see yourself in a few years?" and I would draw a blank. It was easier to express someone else's dreams—like those of my partner—than to articulate my own. It is a sobering realization when you are more at ease with uncertainty than with the discomfort of self-reflection.

Consider how overwhelming it can be to choose a place to live. The world offers nearly 200 countries; even if you have decided to stay within the U.S., there are still 50 states and countless towns and cities. The sheer number of options can be paralyzing. Now, imagine not even knowing what type of neighborhood you want. How would you recognize the right place if you saw it?

But what if you began with a straightforward question: "What do I want?" Try this: Sit quietly and allow yourself to ponder this question for a few minutes. Write down whatever comes to mind. It does not matter if it seems trivial, outlandish, or overly simple. The important thing is that it is genuinely yours.

If this feels challenging, that is perfectly normal. It is difficult to know what you want when you have spent so much time ignoring your desires. Start by identifying what you do not want, which can often be easier. Write these down. Then, take a moment to look at your list. For everything you do not want, ask yourself what you would prefer instead. This exercise is not just a one-time task; it is an ongoing dialogue with yourself as your needs and dreams evolve.

For example, if the thought of interacting with your manager fills you with anxiety, you might wish to feel poised and confident in their presence. If you are dissatisfied with your health, envision a lifestyle where you feel vibrant and strong. Transform each negative feeling into a positive vision of what could be.

This process of self-reflection is not about making perfect choices; it is about understanding your preferences and giving yourself the power to choose. Every "no" to one option is a "yes" to another, actively steering the direction of your life.

As you continue this exploration, remember that your desires might change over time, and that is a natural part of growth. You are not seeking a static answer but engaging in an ongoing dialogue with yourself about who you are and who you aspire to be. This is not about becoming "better" in a conventional sense, but about making choices that reflect your true self.

The path to self-discovery is rarely straight; it is a winding road that requires continual adjustment and reassessment. However, every step you take on this path brings you closer to a life that truly feels like your own.

Transforming Your Inner Dialogue

Embrace the idea that every thought, reaction, and action—even those that seem counterproductive—are inherently aligned with your deeper needs. This perspective is rooted in the belief that there are no adversaries within you, only misunderstood allies. For example, the critical voice that raises doubt about your worth is not your enemy; it is a misguided protector trying to shield you from disappointment or hurt.

Consider a scenario common among trauma survivors, such as those who have experienced sexual abuse. Some may gain weight, and while this might seem self-sabotaging on the surface, it is actually a profound act of self-preservation. The extra weight can subconsciously serve as a barrier, making them feel safer and less vulnerable. Recognizing such behaviors as protective rather than destructive allows us to approach ourselves with greater empathy and understanding.

Once you uncover the underlying motives behind your behaviors—often centered around basic needs like security and acceptance—it becomes easier to respond to them with kindness rather than criticism. This shift is crucial as you contemplate the future you wish to shape.

I remember a conversation I had years back with a close friend. I was habitually harsh on myself, often jokingly, but sometimes to deflect blame or guilt. During one such moment, my friend interjected, saying, "Stop! I would not let anyone talk about my friend that way." This moment of clarity highlighted the harshness of my self-dialogue.

Why is it that we can offer boundless empathy to others but ration it when it comes to ourselves? If it sounds unthinkable to let a loved one demean themselves, why should it be acceptable for us? Turning this compassion inward is transformative, fostering a healthier self-relationship.

Here is how you can cultivate self-compassion:

- **Prioritize Kindness Over Judgment:** In life, mistakes are bound to happen; they are an inherent part of the human experience. Instead of harshly criticizing yourself for these slip-ups, choose to approach them with compassion and understanding. View your imperfections not as shortcomings but as natural facets of being human.
- **Foster Connections Over Isolation:** It is essential to recognize that feelings of inadequacy and self-criticism are not unique to you. Many others share these emotions silently. Understanding this universality can offer solace during moments of self-doubt, reminding you that you are not alone in your struggles.
- **Cultivate Mindfulness Over Identification:** By practicing mindfulness, you can observe your thoughts and emotions without attaching yourself to them. This sense of detachment enables you to recognize that while you may experience certain emotions or behaviors, they do not define your entire identity. This realization empowers you to influence and change these aspects of yourself without compromising your self-worth.

This gentle, introspective approach does not seek to excuse negative behaviors or patterns but rather to address them with the same compassion you would offer to a cherished friend. It is a commitment to nurturing yourself with the same care and kindness you readily extend to others, empowering you to live a life guided not by chance, but by conscious choice.

Embarking on a personal transformation is an exhilarating journey that does not have to be navigated alone. Surround yourself with allies—friends, family, or mentors—who support your growth and embody the qualities you aspire to. Whether it involves reconnecting with old friends or forging new connections based on shared goals, the relationships you cultivate can profoundly shape your path forward.

In your pursuit of personal growth, it is beneficial to start with small steps. Bring a mentor into your life, someone who embodies the qualities you admire or possesses skills you aspire to acquire. This could be a yoga instructor for enhancing physical and mental well-being, a counselor for navigating emotional challenges, or a fellow enthusiast in a hobby that ignites your passion.

As you integrate these supportive relationships into your daily routine, it is crucial to establish boundaries with those who may not align with your evolving journey. This might involve politely declining invitations that no longer resonate with you or stepping back from relationships that drain your energy. Remember, it is not about abruptly cutting ties but rather about consciously choosing where to invest your emotional and social energy.

Surrounding yourself with the right circle of support serves as both a shield against life's challenges and a catalyst for personal growth and self-discovery. By intentionally selecting who you spend time with, you reinforce your aspirations and expedite your journey toward becoming the best version of yourself. The energy and influence of your chosen companions can elevate you to new heights and inspire you to reach goals that once felt unattainable. Therefore, choose your companions wisely, as they play a significant role in shaping your present and future self.

Levels of Change

Have you ever found yourself believing that a new job or a different relationship could solve lingering problems, only to discover that the same issues persist? This frustrating pattern often arises because changes are made on surface levels without addressing deeper, foundational aspects. To grasp this concept better, we can look at it through the lens of neurological levels, similar to Maslow's hierarchy, where each level supports and impacts the ones above and below it.

The First Level—Environment: Your environment encompasses everything tangible in your surroundings—the place you live, your workspace, the people you interact with daily, and even the layout of your surroundings. For instance, I once sat facing a wall at work, leaving me vulnerable to surprises from my ex-husband. However, simply rearranging my office layout to have a clear view of the entrance significantly reduced my stress levels.

The Second Level—Behavior: Sometimes, altering your environment is not sufficient. Our actions and habitual responses often need adjustment. For example, if changing gyms has not led to weight loss, the issue may lie in persistent, unhelpful behaviors—such as dietary choices post-workout or consistency in exercise routines. Consider Joanne, who struggled to wake up on time despite numerous alarms. The root cause was her nighttime routine, involving energy drinks and late-night online gaming.

The Third Level—Capabilities: Beyond behaviors, the next layer to explore is capabilities or skills. These can be categorized into four types: known skills, recognized gaps, unrecognized skills, and skills entirely unknown. Identifying and honing the right capabilities can be pivotal. For instance, someone might discover leadership skills only when tasked with managing a project. Enhancing capabilities often unveils solutions to persistent issues.

The Fourth Level—Beliefs and Values: Deeper still are the beliefs and values driving our actions. These foundational principles profoundly influence how we engage with the world. If you believe you are inherently bad at math, this belief will hinder your efforts, regardless of external support. Transforming such core beliefs involves introspection and potentially redefining your values. I personally review my value cards annually to ensure they align with my actions and decisions.

The Fifth Level—Identity: At a profound level, identity shapes our existence through self-descriptive statements like "I am" phrases. These self-perceptions deeply impact our behavior. Shifting from "I am not good enough" to "I am capable" requires more than just a change in mindset; it demands consistent reinforcement through daily affirmations and correction of negative self-talk. This transformation is crucial for overcoming deep-seated insecurities and fostering a positive self-image.

The Sixth Level—Spirit: The highest level involves spiritual or existential beliefs governed by higher ethical or spiritual standards. This includes our connection to a larger universe or adherence to personal or religious ethical codes. Changes at this level are profound and necessitate a deep commitment to living by these principles, potentially prompting significant shifts in worldview or lifestyle.

Overcoming Perfectionism

The pursuit of perfection is like chasing a mirage that forever eludes our grasp. Recognizing this reality liberates us from the shackles of unrealistic expectations, allowing for a more balanced and fulfilling approach to life's endeavors. Whether it is relationships, projects, or personal growth, embracing imperfection can lead to greater freedom and creativity.

Consider the journey of an aspiring writer embarking on their first novel. Initially fueled by a fervent desire to craft a literary masterpiece, they pour their heart and soul into each sentence, striving for flawless perfection. However, as the years pass, they find themselves mired in frustration, with only a few incomplete chapters to show for their efforts. The culprit? An unyielding pursuit of perfection that paralyzes their creativity and stifles their progress.

Mistakes and imperfections are not just unavoidable; they are fundamental to our growth and development. They serve as catalysts for improvement, providing invaluable opportunities to refine our skills, deepen our understanding, and hone our craftsmanship. Embracing this iterative process allows us to progress steadily and authentically, evolving into our best selves over time.

Moreover, the relentless pursuit of perfection can have detrimental effects on our mental and physical well-being. The constant pressure to meet impossibly high standards creates a perpetual state of stress, similar to running a marathon with no finish line in sight. This chronic stress takes a toll on both our bodies and minds, leading to exhaustion, burnout, and even serious health issues.

It is essential to acknowledge the impact of perfectionism not only on our current state but also on our inner child—the vulnerable part of ourselves that first encountered societal expectations and learned to navigate them. When we set unrealistic standards or criticize ourselves harshly for perceived failures, we perpetuate this cycle of stress and self-doubt, further straining our mental health and well-being.

Permitting ourselves to stumble is crucial for fostering self-compassion and resilience. It is essential to communicate this message to both our adult selves, with their rational understanding, and our inner child, who may still carry the wounds of past expectations and disappointments. By acknowledging that mistakes are not only forgivable but also inherent to the human experience, we can alleviate the pressure to meet unattainable standards and create a sense of safety within ourselves.

When our inner child feels validated and supported, we cultivate resilience, enabling us to face life's challenges with courage and determination. Embracing our imperfections allows us to navigate obstacles with a sense of grace and humility, knowing that every misstep is an opportunity for growth and learning.

Living with perfectionism is like constantly walking a tightrope, where every misstep feels like a failure to meet unrealistic standards. It is an exhausting and unsustainable way to approach life. However, by recognizing that imperfection is not only normal but also essential to our humanity, we can release ourselves from the burden of perfection and embrace a more balanced and fulfilling existence.

Consider a friend of mine, Alex, who once shared a story from his early career days. He made a mistake in a client report—an honest mistake, but in his company, a big deal. Instead of berating himself, he took it to his mentor, who surprised him by recounting a similar misstep from his own youth. This simple act of sharing transformed Alex's view of his error from a career-ender to a stepping stone. This story illustrates the strength of connecting through our imperfections, reminding us that we are not alone in our struggles.

When it comes to setting goals, it is easy to aim for the stars—like committing to an hour at the gym every day. But is that realistic? And what happens when you miss a day? Instead, start small. Maybe it is just 20 minutes of yoga at home or a quick jog. Small victories build momentum and resilience, so when setbacks happen—and they inevitably will—it is not a catastrophe, it is just a minor setback.

And please, let go of comparisons. Scrolling through social media might give the impression that everyone else has it all figured out, but remember, you are likely only seeing the highlights of someone's life, not the behind-the-scenes struggles. Your journey is unique, and it is perfectly okay if it does not resemble someone else's highlight reel.

Finally, let us reframe negative thoughts. Instead of criticizing yourself for faltering, view each mistake as a learning opportunity. If you flubbed a presentation, rather than thinking, "I bombed that," try, "That did not go as planned, but I will do better next time." Shift self-criticism into self-coaching.

Embracing imperfection is not about lowering standards or settling for mediocrity; it is about acknowledging that perfection is unattainable. It is about striving for excellence on your own terms, and understanding that every stumble is a part of your journey, not the conclusion. So, let us ease up on ourselves—we are all evolving works in progress, and that is absolutely okay.

Dream Big

Embarking on a journey to heal your inner child is like embarking on a profound transformation promising abundant rewards. The heart of this transformative journey lies not just in the process itself, which is inherently fulfilling, but in the concrete changes it brings to your life. Healing your inner child involves reconnecting with neglected or hurt parts of yourself, unlocking a realm of new possibilities through this reconnection.

As you progress along this path, each step forward, no matter how small, deserves celebration. It is crucial to occasionally pause, reflect on your starting point, and acknowledge the progress you have made. This recognition serves as a potent motivator to continue moving forward. Here are some transformative experiences you may encounter on your journey:

- **Heightened Emotional and Physical Awareness:** You become more attuned to your emotions and physical sensations, developing a keen awareness of how your body and mind interact. This heightened awareness allows for better communication of feelings, fostering deeper connections with both others and yourself.
- **Rediscovery of Playfulness:** Making time for play becomes a priority as you rediscover the joy and freedom of playful activities. This infusion of joy and creativity into your daily life often leads to a significant reduction in mood swings, as you learn to approach life's highs and lows with a more balanced perspective.
- **Increased Life Satisfaction:** You will notice an uptick in overall satisfaction with life. Spending time alone or with others becomes more fulfilling because you are more in tune with yourself and more comfortable in your own skin. Ultimately, this journey helps you become the person you have always aspired to be—more complete, content, and in control of your happiness.

Healing your inner child is essentially about acknowledging past pain and forging ahead with a renewed mindset. It is about shifting how you perceive yourself and your experiences. As you learn to nurture your inner child, you unlock a level of personal potential that can make nearly anything feel achievable. So, dare to dream big—because through this profound inner work, you are capable of achieving remarkable things.

Exploring Self-Worth and Childhood

Self-worth frequently finds its foundation in our formative years, heavily influenced by the messages we receive from those closest to us. Caregivers, dealing with their own struggles of self-worth, may inadvertently convey feelings of inadequacy or neglect to affirm our inherent value. Despite any negative or diminishing messages we may have encountered during our upbringing, it is essential to acknowledge that our worth has always been intrinsic. Reflecting on how our childhood experiences and the actions of our caregivers have shaped our current perception of self-worth can provide valuable insight into our emotional landscape. Consider the following:

- *What specific messages about worthiness did you receive from your caregivers or significant adults during your childhood?*
- *How did these messages affect your feelings of self-worth growing up?*
- *Can you identify ways in which your caregivers might have struggled with their own self-worth?*
- *How have the perceptions formed in your early years continued to impact your sense of self-worth today?*

_____

_____

_____

_____

_____

Reflect on a time when you felt unworthy:

- _What did you feel unworthy of receiving or achieving?_
- _Who or what contributed to these feelings of unworthiness?_
- _Create two statements that reaffirm your worthiness in this situation._

Reframing Self-Worth

Identify a piece of negative self-talk that undermines your sense of worth.	Reframe this statement into a positive affirmation that reinforces your inherent worthiness.

Building Self-Compassion

Self-compassion serves as a tender embrace for your inner child, providing the same comfort and empathy you would extend to a cherished friend in distress. Through this practice, you can ease the grip of self-criticism and cultivate a nurturing and affirming connection with your inner self. Here are some prompts crafted to inspire introspection, invite the recognition of emotions, and foster a compassionate attitude toward your inner child:

Identify something you need to forgive yourself for. What is holding you back from self-forgiveness?

_____

_____

_____

Recall a kind act you have performed for someone else recently. What did you do?

_____

_____

_____

Reflect on a trait or quality that others appreciate in you. What do people often compliment you on?

_____

_____

_____

Think about something you are currently putting a lot of effort into. What are you working hard to achieve or improve?

_____
_____
_____

Describe a self-care practice you engage in. How do you take care of your well-being?

_____
_____
_____

Formulate a compassionate statement you can tell yourself during tough times. What reassuring words can help you cope?

_____
_____
_____

Write three things you love about yourself, three things you love about how you treat others, three things you deserve to forgive yourself for, and three things you are learning to love about yourself.

_____
_____
_____
_____

Gratitude

Recognizing and appreciating our own qualities and efforts is essential for enhancing self-esteem. Use this exercise to delve into the aspects of yourself for which you are thankful!

Identify a skill, characteristic, or trait you possess that you are truly grateful for. What makes this quality valuable to you?

_____
_____
_____
_____

Reflect on a challenging situation you have successfully navigated. What strengths did you rely on to overcome this challenge?

_____
_____
_____
_____

Develop two "thank you, self" statements that acknowledge and appreciate your efforts and qualities. For example, "Thank you, self, for having the courage to speak up when it was needed."

_____
_____
_____
_____

Healthy Self-Talk

Continue this exercise transforming negative thoughts into positive affirmations to strengthen your self-esteem

I am a failure.	*Every setback is a setup for a comeback. I am learning and growing.*
Nobody cares about me.	*I am loved, and I have people who care about me.*
I cannot do anything right.	*I am on the path of improvement and getting better every day.*

Exploring Your Strengths

Take a moment to list all of your strengths. What are you good at? What qualities do you possess that you are proud of?

_____
_____
_____
_____
_____

Recall a time when you used one of these strengths to manage a challenging situation or interaction. How did it help you?

_____
_____
_____
_____
_____

Think of an instance where you leveraged a strength to reach a personal or professional goal. What was the outcome?

_____
_____
_____
_____
_____

Exploring Your Perseverance

Review your list of strengths from the previous exercise. Select one and describe how you developed it over time. What challenges did you face, and how did you overcome them to strengthen this attribute?

_____
_____
_____
_____
_____

Identify a strength you would like to enhance or acquire. What steps will you take to develop this skill or quality? How can you intentionally focus on this area moving forward?

_____
_____
_____
_____
_____
_____

A Final Note

Dear reader,

As we conclude this workbook, I hope you have found the exercises and insights within these pages to be valuable tools in your journey toward healing and emotional freedom. Your courage to confront and work through abandonment trauma is not only admirable but an inspiration.

I have written this workbook with the intent to support and guide individuals like you, who are striving to overcome their past and embrace a future filled with peace and self-compassion. If you have found any part of this workbook helpful, I kindly ask you to consider sharing your experience.

Your honest review on Amazon could serve as a guiding light to others in similar situations. It can provide hope and assurance that they are not alone in their struggles. As a self-published author, your feedback not only helps me refine my approach but also significantly impacts the book's reach and ability to help others.

Whether your feedback is positive, negative, or somewhere in between, I deeply value and appreciate your honesty. Your opinion helps others discover this resource, which could change their lives for the better.

Thank you for your time and for sharing your journey. I am grateful for every word you choose to share.

Warm regards,

Samantha

Scan to leave a review on Amazon if you live in the US

Scan to leave a review on Amazon if you live in the UK

Scan to leave a review on Amazon if you live in Canada

Scan to leave a review on Amazon if you live in Australia

Conclusion

Every morning, as you awaken to the rhythm of your own heartbeat, it is as if your inner self is cheering you on, encouraging you to embrace your true potential. Simply by opening this book and engaging with its contents, you have taken a significant step forward in responding to that inner cheer. Take a moment to acknowledge and applaud yourself for this courageous beginning.

Reconnecting with your inner self and engaging in the process of reparenting is not just a therapeutic endeavor; it is a profound transformation that touches the very core of your being. Throughout this book, I have attempted to map out this path with clarity and simplicity, ensuring that you can navigate it with confidence. Remember, revisiting certain sections or exercises is not a setback; rather, it is an integral part of mastering your own personal growth journey.

Healing is not a quick fix; it is a gradual process that requires patience and perseverance. It entails delving into years of suppressed emotions and forgotten aspirations. It calls for bravery as you redefine your sense of self and cultivate a new, nurturing relationship with your inner child—one based on mutual respect and collaboration. This investment of time and effort is priceless, laying the foundation for profound personal transformation.

You are no longer bound by the grip of unchecked emotions or the impulses of your younger self. The tools and strategies shared here empower you to mend those early wounds and step boldly into your full potential.

While the chapters of your early life are fixed and unchangeable, your understanding of their impact can undergo a profound transformation. Armed with this newfound insight, you possess the blueprint to navigate the lingering pain and reactive habits that your past has bestowed upon you. This marks a significant stride forward on your journey.

Keep your gaze fixed on the horizon of your aspirations. Continuously engage with every facet of your history—every age, every phase—recognizing that each has contributed to the strength you possess today. Honor them, embrace them, accept them, and work in harmony with them to craft a future that you actively design and shape.

This is your moment to shine. Let your journey unfold in its own unique and fulfilling way, just as it has for countless others. You are an extraordinary individual, deserving of every opportunity to blossom into the person you are destined to become. Embrace the path ahead with confidence and curiosity, knowing that each step you take brings you closer to your true potential.

About the Author

Samantha Parker is a dedicated author who brings her personal experiences and extensive research to the forefront of helping others achieve emotional freedom. Her work aims to support readers in recognizing and addressing abandonment trauma, empowering them to reclaim control over their emotional lives.

Growing up in an environment that presented unique emotional challenges, Samantha learned firsthand the impact of unresolved childhood issues on adult behavior. These experiences became the catalyst for her deep dive into understanding the nuances of emotional healing and recovery. Through years of studying and personal growth, she has developed practical strategies to help others identify symptoms of past trauma and move forward toward healing.

Her approach is both compassionate and pragmatic, focusing on making the tools for recovery accessible to all. Samantha's dedication to sharing her knowledge stems from her own journey of transformation, which she openly shares to inspire and guide others.

Samantha's commitment extends beyond her writings; she actively engages in seminars and workshops, providing support and education to help individuals navigate their paths to healing. Her aim is not only to educate but to foster a sense of community and understanding among those she works with.